In A Week

Martin Manser is a professional ..... ice-.....  .....
experienced in managing people and projects. He has led
large teams of people to create *The Thematic Reference Bible*
(1996), the award-winning *Collins Bible Companion* (2009)
and the best-selling *Macmillan Student's Dictionary* (1996).
Since 2001, he has been a language trainer and consultant
with national and international companies and organizations,
leading courses on business skills and communications,
report writing, project management and time management.

Website: www.martinmanser.co.uk


*I wish to thank Linda Eley for her careful typing of my manuscript and
Nigel Smith and Ian McLellan for their advice on points in the text.*

# Decision Making
# In A Week

Martin Manser

First published in Great Britain in 2013 by Hodder & Stoughton. An Hachette UK company.

This edition published in 2016 by John Murray Learning

Copyright © Martin H. Manser 2013, 2016

*British Library Cataloguing in Publication Data:* a catalogue record for this title is available from the British Library.

*Library of Congress Catalog Card Number:* on file.

Paperback ISBN 978 1473 60950 1

eBook ISBN 978 1444 18042 8

1

The publisher has used its best endeavours to ensure that any website addresses referred to in this book are correct and active at the time of going to press. However, the publisher and the author have no responsibility for the websites and can make no guarantee that a site will remain live or that the content will remain relevant, decent or appropriate.

The publisher has made every effort to mark as such all words which it believes to be trademarks. The publisher should also like to make it clear that the presence of a word in the book, whether marked or unmarked, in no way affects its legal status as a trademark.

Every reasonable effort has been made by the publisher to trace the copyright holders of material in this book. Any errors or omissions should be notified in writing to the publisher, who will endeavour to rectify the situation for any reprints and future editions.

Printed and bound in Great Britain by CPI Group (UK) Ltd, Croydon, CR0 4YY.

are natural, renewable made from wood grown in sustainable forests. g processes are expected to conform to the environmental regulations of the country of origin.

# Contents

# Introduction

You make decisions all the time in everyday life: what to eat, what clothes to wear, with whom you spend your leisure time and how you spend your money. In your business life you are also constantly making decisions, and this decision-making process is the subject of this book: the different activities you – and your business colleagues – need to carry out in order to arrive at a sound decision.

At work, you are deciding how to spend your time, which emails to answer, what subjects to raise at a meeting, when is the best time for your company to launch a new product, what companies you should invest in, what you are not willing to compromise on in negotiations, what policies to develop and how best to market your products and services. Some of these decisions may have already been made for you by other colleagues, usually those above you in your company or organization, and your task is merely to implement them. In other matters, however, you can exercise some control over the actual decision-making process.

To expand on this, we will explore the following:

- **Sunday: Know your aims clearly** What are you actually making a decision about?
- **Monday: Collect relevant information** Consider all the relevant factors as you gather the information you need.
- **Tuesday: Identify different options** Widen your thinking, challenge assumptions and consider creative solutions.
- **Wednesday: Work effectively as a team** Make decisions as a group so that colleagues will feel motivated to implement the decision.
- **Thursday: Evaluate different options** Set objective criteria against which you can examine the various options you have identified.
- **Friday: Make an informed decision** and implement it, communicating it well to all the relevant parties.

- **Saturday: Review the decision carefully**, evaluating the whole decision-making process, noting what went well and learning from mistakes.

Each of the seven chapters, one for each day of the week, covers a different aspect of the decision-making process and starts by introducing the theme for the day. The main part of each chapter explains the key lessons by clarifying important principles, which are backed up by tips and case studies. Each day concludes with a summary, suggestions to follow up and multiple-choice questions to reinforce the learning points.

I have included examples from both the business and the wider sphere of life, as it can be useful to consider how you make decisions outside your work life and then apply those principles to your decision making at work.

The principles I outline here are the fruit of more than 30 years in business, including over 10 years of leading courses on business skills and communications. I have sought to make good decisions and to pass on the results of such decisions to others. My hope is that, as you read and act on what I write, it will be a refresher course that will renew your confidence in your ability to become a more effective decision maker at work.

**Martin Manser**

# SUNDAY

## Know your aims clearly

'Ready, fire, aim.' This anonymous quotation describes how we, all too often, set about things. The right way round is, of course, 'Ready, aim, fire': prepare yourself, know exactly what your target is and then act. Time spent in planning and preparation is time well spent.

Today we lay foundations for making good decisions at work. We begin by asking what it is exactly that a decision needs to be made about. We then move on to consider the following questions:

- What kind of person are you?
  - How would you describe your values, motivation and working style? These will affect the decisions you make at work.
- Do you know your own style?
  - Are you by personality decisive or indecisive? Perhaps the reason you are reading this book is that you are indecisive: you need to realize that by not making a decision you are also in fact making a decision!
- Are you more logical or more creative?
  - What is your own preferred learning style?

Knowing the answers to these questions will help prepare the way for you to make good decisions.

# What is the real decision?

Suppose your company wants to refresh its website. The original website was put together hurriedly a few years ago when everyone suddenly discovered the Internet and realized that they needed a web presence. One of the managers in your company at that time knew that the husband of one of the secretaries understood a little about the web and asked him to build a website. The result is acceptable but the website is ordinary and unimaginative and now looks dated. The subject of refreshing the website has recently come up at meeting after meeting. Frankly, you're a little tired of that, so you decide that you will act on it. After all, you know a couple of friends who could do with the cash and could do a good job.

So you chat with your friends ... and then one of them asks you, 'What is your website for?' This makes you think and you suddenly realize that you don't really know. There's been no discussion, let alone agreement, on the aims of your company's website.

You may say that your company's or organization's website is your 'shop window', but what exactly do you mean by that?

SUNDAY

MONDAY

TUESDAY

WEDNESDAY

THURSDAY

FRIDAY

SATURDAY

Your website may show the location of your offices, with information about your goods or services, but what else do you want it to do? An essential first step is that you clarify the exact aims of your website. You will therefore need to ask yourself some questions, such as:

- Will customers buy direct from us or via a retailer or other intermediary?
- How do we want interested users of our website to respond to us?
- If users want to complain about our service, do we want to make it easy or difficult for them to do so?
- Do we want to promote something – such as an author or a rock band – or inspire users by our choice of photographs, stories or poems?
- Do we want to inform or educate users about a particular need or hobby?
- Do we want to ask users to give money towards our cause?

The first rule in decision making is to ask yourself what exactly you are making a decision about. You need to identify as clearly and precisely as you can what your goal is: what are you trying to decide?

**TIP** *The first rule in decision making is to ask, 'What exactly am I making the decision about?'*

Defining exactly what you need to make a decision about will not come easily. You will need to discuss this with your colleagues. When I say discuss, I mean talk – not email! We need to hear and see the challenge from others as we talk about a subject. Gradually, and over time, you will hone – sharpen, make more focused – what exactly the decision is. In the above example, the primary decision wasn't about 'Who should we ask to refresh our website?' but 'What is our website for?'

> ### *'Nothing is more difficult, and therefore more precious, than to be able to decide.'*
> Napoleon Bonaparte, military and political leader (1769–1821)

## Other factors in the decision

As you begin to focus on the core issue of the decision, other factors will begin to emerge, for example:

- What is the **budget?** (See also Monday.)
- What is the **timescale?**
  - See if you can break down the time factor. Does a decision need to be made quickly? Often the answer is yes, but you need to consider the long-term implications of a rushed decision, especially if it turns out to be the wrong one.
  - If you are introducing change management, you will be faced by cries of resistance: 'We've done it this way for years; why do we need to change?' You need to explain why changes are being made and why this is a good time to begin to make such changes.

- As you may have only one opportunity to make a decision, you need to ensure that it is the right one and that it is made properly. For example, a Member of Parliament once told me that they have many policies they could pursue but that an important part of their party's thinking was to discern what would be most acceptable at any given time.
- You may need to ask for more facts (see also Monday).
- In determining an ultimate goal, you will identify milestones along the way. For example, my son Ben wanted to live in Japan, so this meant that he wanted to learn Japanese. Such a goal was realized practically as a Japanese friend of my wife's gave him lessons every Thursday evening for two years. Visualizing his goal constantly kept him going even during the times when learning the language was demanding and laborious.
- You may need to ask for more time in order for you to reach a decision. In negotiations, you can say, 'I need a little time to think about that.'
- What **secondary matters** can you resolve at the same time?
  - For example, if you are redesigning your website, can you also redesign the company logo at the same time? It is important, however, to keep such secondary matters separate from the main focus of your decision making.

At this stage, don't discount any aim or thought because it is limited. Here, you are 'dreaming dreams' and 'thinking outside the box'. You are looking at creative ways of solving problems and, indeed, of turning problems into opportunities.

If you want to solve a problem, you need to get to the root of it:

1 Think; discuss it with other colleagues; analyse the problem by separating it into its parts to help you define it more closely and understand it more fully.
2 Concentrate on the causes of the problem, not on its symptoms or effects. If someone's work is below standard,

for example, don't keep moaning about it by giving examples, but try to find out why. Ask whether they need training or whether they would be more suitable for a different kind of work.

3 Keep on asking questions, especially the question 'Why?' so that you gain a complete understanding of the real issue. At this stage, it's more about asking the right questions than finding the right answers.

As you begin to list various factors in the decision, you will begin to realize what the decision is *not* primarily about. Again, to use the example above, the decision about a website was not primarily about who was to make the changes but what the purpose of the website was.

# Know what kind of person you are

It is good to stand back, as you begin to consider the foundations of decision making, and analyse what kind of person you are in terms of your:

● morals and principles
● standards of work
● motivation and attitude
● working style.

Answer the following questions to help you find out.

| What kind of person are you? | |
| --- | --- |
| **Morals and principles** | • How honest and responsible are you?<br>• Do you do what you know is right?<br>• Do you always act fairly towards others, respecting them, or do you take unfair advantage of them?<br>• What other values do you and your company or organization hold that you seek to follow in your working life?<br>• Would you make a decision that is wrong for the sake of making a short-term gain?<br>• Are your procedures honest and open to scrutiny? |
| **Standards of work** | • Do you always do your work consistently well or are you often satisfied with a task that you know you have not completed properly?<br>• Do you persevere with a task or do you give up quickly?<br>• Are you committed to excellence? |
| **Motivation and attitude** | • Are you enthusiastic or half-hearted?<br>• Are you diligent or lazy? |
| **Working style** | • Are you content with simply working efficiently, not wasting resources of time and money, or are you also concerned to work effectively, to do the right thing to the best of your ability?<br>• Do you work well with others or are there often areas of conflict?<br>• Do you set priorities and stick to them or are you constantly dealing with crises so that you don't get round to doing what you really should be doing? |

# Doing what is right

Oliver's first job was in an agricultural business, where he soon found that he had a natural flair for sales. Customers would often arrive with a worn-out item such as a lawnmower and expect a generous trade-in allowance against a new one.

The farming customers consistently drove a hard bargain, and none more so than Sam. Sam had the ability to get what he wanted and would almost intimidate staff to secure the best possible price ... and Oliver was to be no exception.

Sam arrived late one day (when all Oliver's senior colleagues had gone home) with a worthless trade-in. After demanding an inflated trade-in allowance, Sam set about seeking generous discount levels. Oliver did his best to hold out and, when the price was finally agreed, he was relieved to have done a deal without making a loss.

Later, when going over the figures, Oliver noticed that he had made a mistake: he had supplied Sam with a basic model mower but charged him for a more expensive one with more features. The result was a reasonable profit and so natural justice seemed to have been done.

However, that night Oliver's conscience set to work as he went over the day's events. He tried to justify what he had done ('unscrupulous customer', 'reasonable profit', 'best for the company', 'too late to change it' and so on) but, whichever way he looked at things, he still knew it was wrong to have overcharged Sam. He wondered what would happen if he owned up to the boss; would he be punished? He worried about his boss's reaction, and thought he might just keep quiet; after all, no one would ever know and so no harm would be done.

Still troubled, however, Oliver owned up the next day, and his boss's argument was simple: 'Do what's right. Credit the customer and don't worry about the profit. The company's reputation is too important.' Humbled and relieved, Oliver had learned a lesson. He phoned the customer, who appeared a little stunned, but Oliver's conscience was clear ... and Sam always seemed a little more amenable after that.

In the above case study, what if Oliver had kept silent? What if his boss had pressurized him into doing wrong? Whether it's big business or a family firm, there is always a cost to doing what you know is right and a temptation to do well for the company in a way that is in fact wrong. You should do what you know is right, even when it is difficult and even costly for the company you work for.

# Know your own style

> *'We know what happens to people who stay in the middle of the road. They get run over.'*
>
> Aneurin Bevan, British statesman (1897–1960)

Think about your own ability to make decisions.

- Are you cautious?
  You may be unwilling to take risks and so put off making a decision, perhaps hoping that the need to make a decision will go away.
- Are you rash?
  If you make decisions quickly, you may not spend time examining all the various factors and risks, so your decisions often turn out to be wrong.
- Do you take a long time to make decisions?
  If you take the time to consider carefully all the various factors and consequences, they often turn out well.
- Do you often 'go round in circles'?
  If you waste a lot of time thinking about all the different aspects of an issue, you may never actually arrive at a point where you come to a decision.

# Know how your brain works

Being aware of how your brain works can help you make more effective decisions. Generally, we can say that the left-hand side of the brain is the more logical side and the right-hand side of the brain is the more creative.

## Being indecisive

Being indecisive is illustrated by the philosophical position known as Buridan's ass. In the example, a hungry donkey stands an equal distance between two identical bales of hay. He starves to death, however, because there is no reason why he should choose to eat one bale rather than the other. The dilemma is said to show the indecisiveness of the will when faced with two equal alternatives. The philosophical example is associated with the French philosopher Jean Buridan (c.1295–1356), although it was first found in the philosophy of Aristotle.

In some people, one side of the brain is more dominant than the other.

- People whose logical (left side) is more dominant deal with information in a linear sequence, tend to be organized and are able to analyse and process words, numbers, facts and other detailed information comparatively easily.
- People whose creative (right side) is more dominant are relatively artistic and imaginative and are used to thinking more visually, intuitively and spatially.

This is a good reason to ensure that you have a mix of both logical and creative thinkers in your decision-making team.

In decision making you may need to adapt your natural way of thinking. If naturally your logical (left side) is more dominant, it can be helpful to work at being more creative, imaginative and intuitive and consider being less cautious and take more risks in decision making. Similarly, if your natural tendency is for your creative (right side) to be more dominant, then it can be helpful to work at being more detailed, analytical and organized, and undertake more long-term planning.

## Know your learning style

Each of us learns differently. Three main types of learner have been identified:

- **visual learners:** those who 'see' things more in pictures, images, diagrams and written text
- **auditory learners:** those who learn by listening and discussing with others
- **kinaesthetic learners:** those who learn by doing, for example through role play, and who are 'in touch with' their feelings.

Again, it can be very useful to make sure you have colleagues with a variety of different learning styles to help you make decisions. Similarly, if you are used to one learning style, it can be helpful to identify that and see whether you can extend your own range to include a greater diversity.

# Skills in decision making

### *'I'll give you a definite maybe.'*
Attributed to Sam Goldwyn, film producer (1879–1974)

Finally today, we open up the dynamics of the skills included in decision making: analysing, synthesizing and evaluating.

- **Analysing**
  This means breaking a task or process down into its constituent parts, often in a logical order. For example, to analyse what the real matter is that needs to be decided means asking and answering the basic question words *who, why, where, when, how, what*. Of these, 'Why ...?' is the most significant one to ask – as in the example earlier today: 'Why do we need a website?' Those whose left (logical) side of the brain is more dominant will find this aspect relatively easy. For more on gathering information, see Monday.

## ● Synthesizing

This is putting the bits back together after you have analysed them (broken them up), or even not analysing them in the first place but seeing things as wholes. This way of thinking sees ideas not as things that need analysing but more like seeds that grow. Those whose right (creative) side of the brain is more dominant will find this aspect relatively easy. For more on identifying different options, see Tuesday.

## ● Evaluating .

This is weighing up the significance of different options, putting a value on something. This can be subjective but it also means that you will probably draw on the specialist technical experience of experts who know the subject matter better than you and who can advise you. For more on evaluating different options, see Thursday.

# Summary

SUNDAY

MONDAY

TUESDAY

WEDNESDAY

THURSDAY

FRIDAY

SATURDAY

Today you learned what questions to ask to help you make good decisions, and about the factors that affect the decision-making process. You need to be able to identify the real issue that you need to make a decision about, along with the secondary issues. You also need to consider the timescale for making the decision and whether it is realistic and, if it is not, how to work out a strategy to seek more time. The kind of person you are is also a factor in decision making, especially in terms of your values and what motivates you at work and the way you work. You'll need to take account of aspects of your personality and what your learning style is, because they also affect the way you make decisions.

### Follow-up

Think about a decision you need to make in the next few weeks.

1 What is the real issue and what are the secondary issues?
2 List five values that you seek to hold that will help inform your decision.
3 Are you by personality cautious or rash; do you want to change such a trait?

# Fact-check [answers at the back]

1. How important is knowing the core issue that you need to make a decision about?
   a) Nice to have ❏
   b) A luxury ❏
   c) A waste of time ❏
   d) Essential ❏

2. When preparing to make a decision, how often should you spend time working out the core issue you need to decide, as distinct from secondary issues?
   a) Occasionally ❏
   b) If I feel like it ❏
   c) If I remember ❏
   d) Always ❏

3. In preparing to make a decision, what do you also need to think about?
   a) Lunch and going to the bank ❏
   b) My annual appraisal ❏
   c) The timescale and budget ❏
   d) Evaluating the decision ❏

4. What should you think about when calculating the time needed to implement a decision?
   a) Doodling to pass the time away ❏
   b) Identifying intermediate milestones ❏
   c) Being promoted ❏
   d) Evaluating the decision ❏

5. When should you take risks in making decisions that you know may get you into trouble?
   a) When I think I can get away with it ❏
   b) Sometimes ❏
   c) Often ❏
   d) Never ❏

6. What is the purpose of the values you hold in life?
   a) To support and provide a firm basis for my actions ❏
   b) I've never even thought about them ❏
   c) To spend my time thinking about them but not doing anything with them ❏
   d) What do you mean by 'values'? ❏

7. When should you try to uphold the values of your company or organization?
   a) When I feel like it ❏
   b) When it's convenient ❏
   c) Constantly ❏
   d) What are our values? ❏

8. How should you use your natural tendency in making decisions, e.g. being cautious or rash?
   a) Always act like that ❏
   b) Try to do the opposite ❏
   c) Be willing to consider changing that way ❏
   d) Not bother changing ❏

9. How should you involve colleagues in the decision-making process?
   a) Only on Mondays ❑
   b) Often, to gain balanced views ❑
   c) When I feel like it ❑
   d) Never ❑

10. What's the best way to make a decision?
    a) Just make it ❑
    b) Separate the tasks of analysing the core issue and of evaluating the options ❑
    c) Ask other people to make it ❑
    d) Analyse the different options but let someone else make the decision ❑

SUNDAY

MONDAY

TUESDAY

WEDNESDAY

THURSDAY

FRIDAY

SATURDAY

# MONDAY

## Collect relevant information

Yesterday we began to establish some ground rules for the whole decision-making process. Today we move on to consider the gathering of relevant information. This is an essential step that will enable you to identify and later evaluate different options to help you come to an informed decision.

Today we will look at:

- understanding the context by asking questions: for example, why the decision needs to be made; who needs to make the decision; who will implement the decision; who will be affected by the decision; and by when the decision needs to be made
- gathering different kinds of relevant information, including consulting experts and undertaking research from a wide range of sources
- working on your costs: knowing how much your time costs and how long tasks take, and drawing up a budget
- reading and understanding statistics.

# Understand the context

Every important decision you make has its own context: it is set in a particular situation. Considering as many of these background factors as possible is an important first step in gathering information.

One good way of helping you start thinking about the context of a decision is to draw a pattern diagram (also known as a 'mind map'). Take a blank piece of A4 paper. Arrange it in landscape position and write in the middle the core issue that you identified on Sunday. (Write a word or phrase, but not a whole sentence.) You may find it helpful to work in pencil so that you can rub out what you write if necessary.

Now write around your central word(s) the different key aspects that come to your mind. You do not need to list ideas in order of importance; simply write them down. To begin with, you do not need to join the ideas up with lines linking connected items.

If you get stuck at any point, ask yourself the question words *why, how, what, who, when, where*, and *how much*. These may well set you thinking.

When I do this, two things often amaze me:

1  how easy the task is; it doesn't feel like work! The ideas and concepts seem to flow naturally and spontaneously. I think this is partly because at this stage I am not trying to put the ideas in any order.
2  how valuable that piece of paper is. I have captured all (or at least some or many) of the key points. I don't want to lose that piece of paper!

Suppose you need to make a decision about installing a new computer system at work. Your diagram might look like the one below. You are not trying to make a decision at this point, and you should avoid the temptation to do so. You are simply listing different aspects of the issue that could be relevant factors.

The example shown is a general one, and you could add a lot more detail under each point. For instance, the bullet point under **Time available** is 'Should be ready for 1 January' and

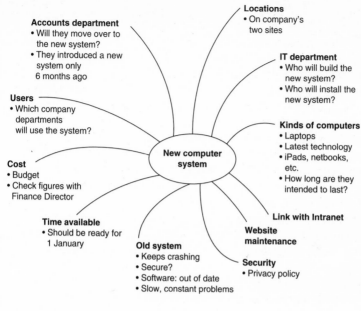

SUNDAY
MONDAY
TUESDAY
WEDNESDAY
THURSDAY
FRIDAY
SATURDAY

you could expand this to include various milestones related to time and schedule, such as:

| | |
|---|---|
| Gather data | June–August |
| Identify options | by 15 September |
| Shortlist the three most likely solutions | by 1 October |
| Agree best solution | by 15 October |
| Approach top company | by 1 November |

To pursue this further, here are some questions you could ask to get you thinking.

- **Why** does the decision need to be made?
- **Who** are the key people involved?
- **Who** are the best colleagues to implement the decision?
- **Who** will make the decision?
- **Who** will be affected by the decision?
  Will colleagues – or you – need to be trained in new skills?
  If you are dealing with a professional business matter, think

about how that affects your personal life outside work. For example, if you are being asked to relocate or undertake a job that involves being away from home for four nights every week, think about how this will affect your home life.

- **What** are the different competitive products?
  It's useful to compare different items, for example different solutions or types of new computer software to replace your existing ones.

- **How** does the problem express itself?
  You could draw a flow chart to show the various different stages that led to the problem, how the problem is expressed (its symptoms) and the connections between the problem's causes and effects.

- **How** will you measure the success of the results of your decision?
  Be as objective as you can. Will the new system be less disruptive to business? Will it produce fewer computer crashes and fewer calls to helplines?

- **When** will you need to make the decision?
  You will need to determine the intermediate stages you must complete to reach this point and the dates by when they need to be completed. For example, if you are recruiting new staff, work out a timetable for the various different elements of the task, beginning at the end, that is, the ideal date when you want the person to start employment. Work backwards from that date to now, including the following stages: agreeing the job description, person specification and method of application; advertising the post; allowing time for applications; working out how to deal with references; shortlisting; interviews; offer of job and acceptance of offer; and issuing contract.

- **Where** are the relevant factors located?
  Is space an issue? Would buying and installing certain software need you to change offices or even rent new offices?

Now is the time to question assumptions, for example about the perceived limitations of your role or about a possible new direction for your company. Think big! Do you need to think differently about how you will market your company and let the 'outside world' know of your existence?

# PESTLE and SWOT analyses

PESTLE and SWOT are two acronyms for techniques to help you understand the context of the decision you have to make by examining a range of factors.

PESTLE analysis

| **P**olitical changes | Changes in government, e.g. consideration of the effects of war |
|---|---|
| **E**conomic changes | Is the economy in a recession or is it growing? Is your market expanding? What is the level of your potential customers' disposable income? |
| **S**ociological changes | Is the birth rate increasing? What changes in lifestyles are there? How socially mobile are your potential customers? |
| **T**echnological changes | The latest innovations in the digital market, e.g. smartphones, tablets |
| **L**egal changes | Changes in the law, in regulatory bodies or in regulations, e.g. health & safety |
| **E**nvironmental changes | The effects on your carbon footprint |

Considering these external influences on your business will help you put your decision in a wider context.

SWOT analysis

| **S**trengths | What are you better at than your competitors? What is your USP (unique selling point)? |
|---|---|
| **W**eaknesses | What do your competitors perceive as your weaknesses? Is morale low? Is your leadership committed? Are there gaps in the skills of your colleagues? |
| **O**pportunities | What changes in the market or changes in lifestyle can you exploit to maximize your profits? |
| **T**hreats | Is the market for your product declining? Are key colleagues on the verge of leaving? Is your financial backing stable? |

Conducting a SWOT analysis to analyse where your company/organization is now will help you make the decision before you.

# Gather relevant information

By looking at the context of a decision, you are beginning to gather relevant information. You can build on what you have thought so far by undertaking research in several ways.

You can carry out some initial research by asking questions. Build on the information you have collected in your pattern diagram. Go back to the question words we discussed earlier today: *why, how, what, who, when, where* and *how much.*

You will already have some of the information you need, but you should now conduct research to gather enough information to enable you to make an informed decision.

Make a list of the following details:

1 the information you need
2 the sources of such information, such as:
   - colleagues
   - former colleagues with a good working knowledge of the field
   - friends
   - the Internet, via a search engine
   - specialist magazines or periodicals
   - books – don't ignore these; not everything in the history of the world is available digitally
   - industry-specific data and information

- experts – a search on the Internet may well reveal experts' websites and a well-worded email may elicit some help
- a coach or mentor to offer more general guidance

3 the timescale by which you need to have gathered this information.

You could put this in table form, as shown here. This is based on today being 1 May.

Information-gathering timescale

| Information needed | Source of information | Timescale to have information by |
|---|---|---|
| Range of new software: positive and negative features | Colleagues, former colleagues and friends | end May |
| | Internet | end May |
| | Specialist periodicals | end June |
| | Books | end June |
| | Industry-specific data | end June |
| | Experts | end June |
| | Coach/mentor | at monthly meeting: 15 May |

It can be helpful to gather as much relevant objective data as possible, for example the number of computer crashes in a given period or the number of calls made to a computer helpdesk. Such data can support your choice of a certain type of computer software as a replacement.

## Available or relevant?

A lot of information will be available. In fact, since the advent of the Internet, you probably have access to too much information. What comes with experience is knowing which information is relevant, closely connected to the matter you need to make a decision on.

Gather information about the extent of a problem. For example, if the quality of a product is failing, does this affect 1 in 1,000 products or 900 in 1,000?

# Work on your costs

Sooner or later, money comes into your decision making.

On many of the courses I lead, the words 'money', 'figures' or 'math[s]' evoke a reaction in some participants of 'I don't do math[s]' or 'I'm no good with figures'. A few delegates are skilled in this area and enjoy figures, relishing their ability to do mental arithmetic in their head, but many colleagues are not. But the hard truth is that you've got to have some grasp of math[s] to make business decisions. Decisions nearly always include the money factor, so you need to get used to that fact sooner rather than later.

Fortunately, we can break down what you need to understand into some basics: knowing your own costs, knowing how much time tasks take, and drawing up a budget.

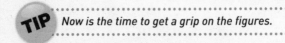

**TIP** *Now is the time to get a grip on the figures.*

## Know your own costs

What we want to work out here is how much you cost your company or organization. This is different from how much you are paid, as we shall see.

Suppose you earn £20,000 per year. If we divide this figure by the number of days you work productively, i.e. omitting holidays and allowing for illness, this could give, say, 46 weeks per year. £20,000 ÷ 46 = £434.78 per week or £86.96 per day, assuming five days per week. If we then divide this figure by the time per day you spend on productive work, say two-thirds of seven hours (= 4.66 hours), we come to £18.66 per hour: this is the amount that you are paid per hour gross, i.e. before tax and other deductions.

That is only half the story, however. Your actual cost to your company or organization is about twice that figure. This is to allow for the overheads of the company, which include the general business expenses, the taxes it pays as an employer, the rent of offices, and heating, power and water. So the cost to your company or organization of employing you is £18.66 × 2 = £37.32 per hour.

On this basis, if a business meeting lasts seven hours and is attended by six colleagues, the cost of that meeting to the company or organization is 7 x 6 x £37.32 = £1,567.44, which is probably considerably more than you thought.

## Know how much time tasks take

As mentioned above, the time you spend doing productive work is only a proportion of the total time you spend at work. This productive work comprises the main tasks that your job involves, especially those tasks that produce actual income. Saying that some work is productive implies at least three things:

1 Some of your time is productive and some is unproductive.
2 You know the difference between your productive time and your unproductive time.
3 You know how much time you are spending productively and unproductively.

Today, for example, my tasks are:

● to write this chapter – I know from experience that writing each chapter of this book takes about two good mornings' work (I know I work better in the morning so I reserve mornings for productive work)

- to read back through the draft of my previous chapter and make some changes (productive work)
- make some phone calls to chase colleagues; prepare for courses and meetings later this week (unproductive work).

The first two (productive) tasks will probably take me four to five hours. The last (unproductive) task will perhaps take me about two hours. In other words, I have some grip on my time: I am managing it.

Interruptions will probably come: a delivery of stationery is due this morning; I will check and answer emails at certain times through the day. Overall, however, I exercise some control over my time. I keep a log of both my productive and my unproductive time so I know how much time writing projects take. I can then work out the hourly rate I need to charge my customers.

If you don't know how long tasks take, don't just pluck a figure out of the air. Try a sample first. For example, you might think that checking 100 items in a list will take you four hours. You try it for half an hour and discover to your horror that you only check two items. Don't be tempted to say that the figure will improve significantly because you will know what you are doing when you come to the actual task. The rate at which you work may improve slightly, but even if you finished checking three items in half an hour, checking 100 will take 16.7 hours (30 minutes divided by 3 = 10 minutes each; 100 × 10 minutes = 1,000 minutes = 16.7 hours), which is more than four times longer than you originally thought.

## Admin takes far longer than you think

Your admin tasks ('unproductive' work) – such as putting in an expense claim, arranging a future meeting with colleagues and making phone calls – are all important but they may not be part of your productive work. You still need to do these tasks, however, to keep your company or organization running smoothly, and it's important to realize that the time they take is probably far longer than you think.

# Draw up a budget

As part of the decision-making process, you will often need to plan a budget. Your aims here are:

1 to list the range of different items of expenditure and income
2 to make the figures as accurate as possible.

I often work on these on a spreadsheet, with columns for 'projected' and 'actual' expenditure and income.

All that you have read above, on costing your time and knowing how much of your time is productive, is significant here. Your aim is not to write down just any figure without thinking about it, but to make sure that the figures you put down are as accurate as possible.

You are in business to make a profit. Even if your company or organization is not for profit, you do not want to make a loss, so you need at least to cover costs. Probably you need to make a profit.

Here is an example of a budget for a training course. The budget is made up of the projected figures under two main headings: costs (expenditure) and income.

A budget for a training course

| Costs | Income | £ |
|---|---|---|
| Speaker | | 4,000 |
| Venue | | 6,000 |
| Marketing | | 3,000 |
| Administration | | 5,000 |
| Office | | 2,000 |
| **Subtotal** | | **20,000** |
| Contingency | | 2,000 |
| **Total costs** | | **22,000** |
| | | |
| | Delegates' fees | 24,000 |
| **Profit** | | **2,000** |

1 Administration costs of £5,000 are for 125 hours at £40 per hour. (This is what the admin personnel costs the company, not what they are paid! See above.)
2 Contingency is the amount included for unforeseen events: about 10 per cent of the total figure is widely used.
3 Income is the amount you need to receive to at least cover your costs.

You need to gather all this information to enable you to make a decision about the price you will charge each delegate.

You can work out the 'break-even' point, the point at which the money you receive covers your costs. The break-even point here is £22,000, so if delegates' fees are £400 each, you will need 55 delegates (55 x £400 = £22,000) to cover costs. If you have more than 55 delegates (in the example shown the income is £24,000, i.e. 60 delegates at £400 each), a profit is made. If you have fewer than 55 delegates, you will make a loss.

---

### Return on investment (ROI)

Return on investment is the percentage return you make over a certain time as a result of undertaking the project. It is calculated according to the formula:

*ROI = (profits [or benefits] ÷ investment [your costs]) x 100*

One way of considering return on investment is to work out the *payback* period, the time taken for the profits or benefits to cover the cost of your investment.

**Example**

A project to train all your staff in report-writing skills might cost £50,000, including the tutor's fee, materials and administration. Its benefits could be measured in terms of savings of work time and productivity increases of £60,000 over one year, so the return on investment is:

$$(60,000 ÷ 50,000 [= 1.2]) \times 100 = 120\%.$$

# Reading statistics

If you are gathering statistical data, check the figures. Use an alternative way from the main way the figures were compiled to verify the data.

Here are some tips on reading and understanding numbers presented in tables.

- **Check the basics:** the dates covered, the sources used, the scale used and the context of the figures. For example, if the figures represent a sample, how large is that sample? Are the assumptions reasonable? Are certain figures omitted? Why? Check the definitions of terms used. Are they sound? If percentages are shown, percentages of what?
- **Understand the data:** take one row or column and think through its content and implications to make sure you understand it.
- **Compare figures:** look at the columns and see if you can discern patterns in the data. Consider any trends: do the numbers show a consistent pattern that increases or decreases? For example, is actual expenditure consistently higher than budgeted?
- **Consider averages:** calculate the average for a particular row or column and see what variations and exceptions there are. Try to work out reasons for such differences, such as variations because of higher or lower income or differing levels of employment.
- **Read the text that accompanies the data:** check that you agree with it and be particularly wary of such words as 'significant' and phrases like 'these figures of course show'.
- **Beware of making assumptions:** be careful about putting too much confidence in making extrapolations of data that assume a trend will continue.

# Summary

Today we discussed the need to collect relevant information. We have thought about the importance of understanding the context of the decision you need to make and of asking questions to help you understand the different factors that make up your decision. We then looked at ways to gather information and at the importance of knowing your costs so that you can draw up an accurate budget.

**Follow-up**

Think of a particular decision you need to make.

1 Draw a diagram to show the different aspects of what you need to make the decision about.

2 If any fresh ideas occurred to you as you drew this up, add them.

3 List the sources of information you need to consult and the dates by which you need to consult those sources.

4 List the different stages you need to complete to make the decision and the dates for completing those stages.

5 Undertake a SWOT analysis of your company or organization.

6 Work out how much you cost your company or organization.

SUNDAY
MONDAY
TUESDAY
WEDNESDAY
THURSDAY
FRIDAY
SATURDAY

# Fact-check [answers at the back]

1. How important is it to understand the context of what you need to make a decision about?
   a) A waste of time: I want to make the decision now ❑
   b) A luxury ❑
   c) Nice to have ❑
   d) Essential ❑

2. From what sources should you gather data?
   a) Only the Internet ❑
   b) A range of sources including colleagues, friends, periodicals and books ❑
   c) So many different sources that I've lost track ❑
   d) The few sources I always trust ❑

3. What do the letters in PESTLE stand for?
   a) Products, experience, service, targets, loyalty, energy ❑
   b) Profits, ethics, selling, teamwork, leadership, empowerment ❑
   c) Political, economic, sociological, technological, legal, environmental ❑
   d) Political, economic, structure, technology, literacy, employees ❑

4. What do the letters in SWOT stand for?
   a) Structure, what if, organizing, thinking ❑
   b) Strengths, weaknesses, opportunities, threats ❑
   c) Strategy, wealth, objectives, trust ❑
   d) Sales, win–win, operations, teamworking ❑

5. What is the best way to undertake research?
   a) When I feel like it ❑
   b) It's not that important ❑
   c) Carelessly ❑
   d) Methodically ❑

6. How should you keep track of time spent on different aspects of your work?
   a) When I remember ❑
   b) Constantly ❑
   c) Never ❑
   d) So often it's hard to do my work ❑

7. What is a key aspect of preparing a budget?
   a) To estimate all the costs and hope they are realistic ❑
   b) To finish it as quickly as possible ❑
   c) To make the figures as accurate as possible ❑
   d) Spending so much time on it that I miss the deadline ❑

8. How important is a contingency in a budget?
   a) Essential ❑
   b) Nice to have ❑
   c) What is contingency? ❑
   d) A luxury ❑

9. What is ROI in the context of costing?
   a) Republic of Ireland ❑
   b) Ratio of interest ❑
   c) Return on investment ❑
   d) Resources of interaction ❑

10. What is the payback period, in the context of costing?
   a) The time taken for the profits or benefits to cover the cost of my investment ❑
   b) My product's costs ❑
   c) The pay I am owed ❑
   d) An act of revenge ❑

# TUESDAY

## Identify different options

You have now learned about two key aspects of the decision-making process. You know exactly what you need to make a decision about and you've started collecting information. Today you can begin to identify the different options that are opening up before you. If you are unclear about the best option to choose and don't know which way to turn, you will be shown different ways to generate alternatives that you could use in your decision making.

Today we shall look at ways to:

- widen your thinking
- challenge assumptions
- concentrate your resources where they will be most effective
- be imaginative, using the SCAMPER technique to help you be more creative
- consider timing
- give your subconscious mind and your intuition the opportunity to do their work and allow fresh ideas to emerge
- move beyond confusion.

# Widen your thinking

You can widen your thinking in various ways. One good way is to meet with colleagues and discuss ideas freely. When discussing ideas, don't be too critical of any idea. Don't limit yourselves. Think of as many different options as possible; build on others' ideas. Explore unlikely – even random – possibilities.

Here are some don'ts to follow as you discuss various possible options.

- Don't pretend you still have to make a decision when you have already made up your mind.
- Don't stick with what you are used to. For example, don't always go with your favourite supplier: see whether other suppliers can offer a better service.
- Don't choose the first option that offers itself. For example, if you move to a new area and are looking for a dentist for your regular check-up, a colleague may recommend theirs. You may then choose that one, even though you haven't undertaken wide research.
- Don't ignore the obvious. The obvious might just be the best option.

- Don't get stuck in the past. Move on to the decision you need to make now. For example, you may already have spent £1,000 replacing the steering wheel on your car and then you have another bill for £1,500. It is important not to let the £1,000 you have already incurred (the 'sunk cost', a cost that you have already spent and which you cannot recover) weigh too heavily in your decision to spend a further £1,500.
- Don't be hopelessly optimistic. You are not a gambler, hoping that roll of the dice must eventually fall in your favour. Don't discern patterns where there aren't any. Don't indulge in wishful thinking but be realistic.
- Don't focus on the wrong issue. A few months ago I decided I needed to sort out all the paper I had amassed during ten years of leading training courses. I kept putting off this task until the pile got unwieldy and I was losing valuable time trying to find papers. When I stopped to think, the core issue wasn't time but having enough space to lay out all the papers while I sorted them out. So I planned a time when my wife was at work and I could spread out all the papers, sort them and throw many away.
- Don't be too cautious. I am naturally quite cautious. I remember leaving my house many years ago to go to a publishing meeting. A little voice inside me said, 'Why are you going? You know nothing will happen.' I made myself go, however, and at the meeting agreed to compile a book that later sold more than 80,000 copies. What if I had listened to my natural cautious self and had not been adventurous? You can be so cautious that you never do anything. What have you always wanted to try? Is now the time to do it? If not now, then when? For example, suppose you want to delegate a task to a colleague. If you wait for that colleague to be absolutely ready to fulfil that task, you might wait for ever. Delegate to colleagues who are nearly ready. After all, were you fully ready when work was first delegated to you?
- Don't delay too long in making a decision. Often, prices for flights, trains, etc., increase as the time for their departure draws near. You will remain more in control – and pay less! – if you decide sooner rather than later.

# Challenge assumptions

When you are generating ideas and coming up with estimates or forecasts, challenge the assumptions you make. For example, yesterday I worked on a schedule for a new project that I am about to start. I thought I knew how long a particular task would take and had estimated it to be about ten hours. It was only when I worked through a sample text that I found far more errors than I thought there would be. I originally thought that the task would take me 15 hours. I then recalculated that the task would probably take about 40 hours, considerably more than my original estimate.

Try to gain definite facts. If you haven't got access to definite facts or statistics, separate the process that you are considering into its constituent parts and test each part to identify what assumptions you are making to see if they are true. The SCAMPER technique described below may be useful here.

● Be prepared to think differently, e.g. be explicit if your present strategy is failing. Face up to the 'elephant in the room', the subject everyone is aware of but that is not discussed because it is too uncomfortable.

- Are you keeping up with (if not in advance of) trends in your industry?
- Don't be afraid to take risks (see also Thursday).

**TIP** *Never be tempted just to guess a number; when estimating and forecasting, remember that your final figures are likely to be nearer the trick of 'think of a number and double it'.*

## Concentrate on what will be most effective

The 80:20 rule, also known as the Pareto principle (or law), is seen, for example, in company sales: 80 per cent of the sales may come from 20 per cent of the customers. The expression derives from the name of the Italian economist and sociologist Vilfredo Pareto (1848–1923).

Pareto worked as a director of Italian railways and a superintendent of mines before becoming a professor of economics in 1892. His studies led him to analyse consumer demand and to formulate a law of the distribution of income within a society.

Pareto's observations, later formulated as the 80:20 rule, have also been applied to spheres outside economics and business; for example, 80 per cent of crime may be committed by 20 per cent of criminals. This has significance: if you want to see a meaningful reduction in crime, you target the 20 per cent of criminals. You concentrate your efforts on where they will really make a difference and have the most effect.

# Be imaginative

Too much of our thinking is often based solely on data and 'information'. Ways to be more imaginative including using the SCAMPER technique and other methods of improving creativity.

# The SCAMPER technique

The SCAMPER technique, first developed by Alex Osborn in his book *Applied Imagination* (1953), offers a set of questions to help you come up with new ideas. It is a useful way to help you produce fresh thoughts about an issue. SCAMPER is an acronym that stands for a series of actions, as shown in the following table.

| Letter | Action | Question | Example |
|--------|--------|----------|---------|
| S | Substitute | Can you look for someone or something as a substitute for a person, product or process? | What happens if we substitute 3.20 p.m. for 3 p.m. as a meeting time? (Perhaps colleagues would arrive at the meeting more promptly.) |
| C | Combine | Can you combine two or more parts to fulfil something different? | Can I combine two different forms that are filled in by two different colleagues into one, to save time? |
| A | Adapt | How could you adapt the functions or appearance of a product? | What would happen if I changed the ketchup container from a glass jar to a plastic bottle? |
| M | Modify | Can you make a significant change to a situation, perhaps in an exaggerated way? | How can I add extra value to my product? |
| P | Put to other use | How can you apply your product elsewhere, or is there an external idea that you can apply to the opportunity you are considering? | What different markets could I sell my product in? |
| E | Eliminate | Can you remove anything superfluous in the product or process? | Can I omit the footnotes in the report I am writing? |
| R | Reverse | Can you swap the order of elements in your process? | What would happen if I began with the needs of my consumer rather than the advantages that I see in my products? |

# Be creative

An example of creative thinking is shown in the 1956 film *The Man Who Never Was*, based on the book of the same name by Ewen Montagu (to whom I am distantly related). Montagu had the idea of deceiving the German forces during the Second World War by planting false information on a dead body that was washed up on the coast of Spain. His plan ('Operation Mincemeat') was effective.

Here are some tips to help increase your creativity.

- **Visualize situations.**
  For example, here is a brief extract from a diary I wrote following a recent visit to China: 'It's Saturday morning ... 25 degrees ... we walk through the park sipping kumquat and lime juice: older folks dancing, a lady balancing several layers of wine glasses on her nose (later, the lady had gone and in her place clowns were performing in front of children), groups of deaf people signing to one another, many people walking, others exercising or doing t'ai chi ... this was our experience a few days ago.'

- **Evoke the senses.**
  When I am stressed, I try to think of one of two situations: hearing the gentle lapping of water on a shore of a lake in Austria or sipping cola in a restaurant in France. Both these situations are memorable because they evoke the senses.

- **Think of television advertisements that stick in your mind.**
  What makes them successful? What are the elements of story?

- **Change your mind; don't stay with your fixed opinions.**
  Alongside all the objective criteria, be prepared to think of the unexpected and to be original, innovative, inventive and adventurous. You could begin by drawing a situation or actively playing it out.

> *'Genius is 10 per cent inspiration and 90 per cent perspiration.'*
>
> Thomas Edison, American inventor (1847–1931)

## My creativity paid off

I remember it now. Our daughter was still in a cot in our old house. I was thinking about words beginning with the letter G. A few were interesting: *galore* (plenty) is an example of an adjective that follows the noun it refers to (*whisky galore!*); *galvanize* (stir into action) is an example of a word named after a person (the 18th-century Italian scientist Luigi Galvani).

I suddenly had a brainwave – what if on every page of a dictionary we could highlight a few words that were remarkable in a distinctive way? Thus the idea came about for a book that I later worked on with my friend and colleague Nigel Turton. It was originally published by Penguin as the *Wordmaster Dictionary* and sold well. It is an 'ordinary' dictionary except that on nearly every page alongside the main entries we highlighted in a boxed panel a particular word with an interesting history, idiom, grammatical feature or point of usage. My creativity paid off!

# Consider timing

Certain events have to come before others. A friend of mine is currently renovating a house. At the start, he thought it would be relatively easy: call a plumber to fix the bathroom, redecorate a few rooms. Then he realized he had to pursue matters in a certain order: hire an architect to produce plans, cost different options, rewire the house ... in fact, the redecorating is one of the last things he has to do.

Timing has to do with the *order* of events. It is obviously also critical when deciding to launch a new product. For example, it would be foolish to begin to think about launching a new toy on to the Christmas market in September. That is far too late because you will want to be selling it in the shops from October/November. You should have begun far earlier.

Are there recurrent seasons in your industry? After a few years as a freelance editor, I noted that May is a significant month in the year for publishers: this is when they turn their attention to the following year's books. Work on their list for publication in September/October is relatively complete by then and they have time to consider the following year. So I have found that publishers are receptive to fresh thinking in May.

A further significant point about timing is to distinguish the short term from the medium and long term. Is your aim to plan only for a short-term success or do you want to build a long-term success for a new product?

## Don't ignore your intuition

'I just know', 'I felt that was right', 'I had a hunch that ...' and 'The thought just came to me.' How often do you use or hear such phrases? Intuition has a role to play in the decision-making process.

Intuition can be defined as 'the power of knowing something without evident reasoning'. There may be no logical explanation for something; you discern the truth about a person or situation and you just know it is right. For me, intuition is important, but it is only one factor in the decision-making process. If I am tired or stressed, my emotions can play havoc with my thinking processes, so I have to be careful.

Intuition is linked to your 'depth mind', your subconscious. It seems that your depth mind digests myriad thoughts – analysing, synthesizing and evaluating them – resulting in an intuitive thought coming to your consciousness.

That is why it is useful to 'sleep on it': sleep for a night before making a significant decision. Sometimes this is plain common sense. I have an informal rule for myself that I do not send out a costing for a project without sleeping on it. A while back I costed a project one day and, when I checked my figures the next day, I realized I had for some inexplicable reason calculated the figure to be only half the correct total, so there is ordinary wisdom as well as intuitive reason behind the need to 'sleep on it'.

Don't ignore the thoughts that occur to you when you are taking a shower or driving home from work and are not thinking about a problem. Allow your subconscious mind the opportunity to do its work and let fresh ideas emerge when you are not thinking about making the decision.

## Something wasn't quite right

From the first meeting, Harry had a gut feeling that something wasn't quite right with the outside supplier, Special Solutions Ltd. Harry's company had accepted the lowest bid and Harry had reservations about that, but he was left to manage the project. When he met regularly with colleagues from Special Solutions, they were pleasant enough – in fact, at times they were too pleasant: it was as if their superficial pleasantness was hiding something below the surface. Sure enough, matters came to a head at the second of their monthly review meetings, when it became clear that Special Solutions had not met their targets for manufacturing and were waiting on one of their suppliers to deliver machines.

The whole matter left Harry with a bad taste in his mouth. Not only did his company have to negotiate a withdrawal from their contract with Special Solutions but they also had to put the contract out for tender again and several months' valuable time was lost. Never again would his company accept a bid simply because it offered the lowest price. In future, Harry knew he would make sure not only that he would consider the objective facts and figures but also that he would listen to his own niggling thoughts, his own intuitive sense.

# Move beyond confusion

Have you ever felt confused in the decision-making process? It is a good sign – it means that you have immersed yourself in the relevant factors well. You may even feel as if you are drowning. From having not enough information you may suddenly feel overwhelmed by having too much information to think about.

Some of the information may conflict with other information: one expert may be strongly in favour of choosing a certain brand of software, whereas reviews on the Internet describe it as weak and underperforming.

You may not know which way to turn – but this is all part of the decision-making process. In fact, you may even think life seemed far simpler before you began having to make this decision! You may want to go back to that time when everything seemed safe and secure.

But you are beginning to change. As you have thought through different approaches, you have begun to wonder. For example, at the same time as installing new computer software to deal with accounts, you may find some software that can also help you as a good project-management tool, so you come up with the idea of achieving two goals at the same time.

 **TIP** *At times you may catch a glimpse of how things might fit together. Capture it by pursuing it before you lose it.*

# Summary

Today we've looked at a range of techniques to help identify different options in your decision making. You have learned how to widen your thinking so that you don't stick with what you are used to or choose the first option that offers itself. You can challenge assumptions, concentrate on what will be most effective, and take timing into account. You have also understood the importance of your imagination and intuition in decision making, and recognized that allowing yourself some confusion can also lead to new ideas and approaches.

## Follow-up

Think of a particular decision you need to make.

1  Be imaginative. Think of different ways of creatively expressing your decision and the options you can choose from. Discuss ideas with colleagues.

2  What is the most imaginative idea you can think of?

3  What assumptions are your options based on?

4  Where does the 80:20 rule apply in your company or organization?

5  How important to you is your intuition?

SUNDAY
MONDAY
TUESDAY
WEDNESDAY
THURSDAY
FRIDAY
SATURDAY

# Fact-check [answers at the back]

1. How often should you identify different options?
   a) Nearly always ❏
   b) Occasionally ❏
   c) Never; I choose according to my gut instinct ❏
   d) Never; I always choose what I've chosen before ❏

2. When you have to decide between something you've chosen up to now and something new, what should you do?
   a) Always choose what I've chosen before ❏
   b) Always choose something new ❏
   c) Toss a coin ❏
   d) Consider choosing what I've not chosen before ❏

3. When making a decision, what should you do?
   a) Consider my personality ❏
   b) Ignore my personality ❏
   c) Toss a coin ❏
   d) Go home early ❏

4. How often do you challenge your assumptions?
   a) Regularly ❏
   b) Occasionally ❏
   c) Never ❏
   d) Always and awkwardly ❏

5. What does the 80:20 rule tell you?
   a) To lose 20 per cent of my body weight ❏
   b) To target my resources so they will be most effective ❏
   c) To have lunch ❏
   d) To exhaust my resources ❏

6. How often should you consider fresh ways of looking at an issue you need to decide?
   a) What's wrong with how I've thought about it before? ❏
   b) Occasionally ❏
   c) Often ❏
   d) Never ❏

7. What do the letters in the SCAMPER technique stand for?
   a) Strategy, communication, alternatives, management, problem solving, emotion, responsibility ❏
   b) Sales, costs, aspirations, marketing, profits, employees, risk ❏
   c) Stakeholders, competition, adaptability, motivation, products, environment, resources ❏
   d) Substitute, combine, adapt, modify, put to other use, eliminate, reverse ❏

52

8. How would you improve your ability to be imaginative?
a) What's 'imaginative?' ❏
b) I don't bother because I don't need it ❏
c) By persevering until I find I am innovative ❏
d) By wondering how much money I could make ❏

9. How important is timing in making a decision?
a) The only matter to think about ❏
b) One significant factor among others ❏
c) Totally irrelevant ❏
d) My boss's problem, not mine ❏

10. How important are intuitive thoughts about a decision?
a) The most important factor ❏
b) One factor to bear in mind ❏
c) An infallible guide ❏
d) A complete waste of time ❏

# WEDNESDAY

# Work effectively as a team

Who makes the decisions in your company or organization? Is it only the managers themselves, or do the managers involve others in the decision-making process?

Today we stand back from the detail of identifying and evaluating options to discuss the making of decisions in teams. We know that when we begin to talk through the different aspects of a matter the real issues become clearer, so today I am going to suggest that it is better if decisions are made by groups.

When a decision is made that affects colleagues, the more they are included in the decision-making process the stronger their motivation will be. When decisions are made by the whole team, there needs to be a balance of different roles within the group, so we will consider different team roles.

Finally today we will look at the forum in which we make decisions – the meeting. We'll consider the need to make good preparations for meetings and how to run them well in order to facilitate the making of good decisions.

# Who makes the decisions in your organization?

What is the dominant style of decision making in your company or organization?

1 **Decisions are made by the leader.**
   - Advantage: considered to be quick and efficient
   - Disadvantage: could be considered ruthless; some colleagues may disagree or not feel valued because their opinion was not sought
2 **Decisions are made by the majority.**
   - Advantage: considered to be fair
   - Disadvantage: could be divisive among colleagues; a minority may not agree and so they may not be willing to give their support to implementing the decision
3 **Decisions are made by general agreement (consensus).**
   - Advantage: as the way forward about a decision becomes apparent from discussion, colleagues will feel valued and will 'own' their involvement in implementing the decisions
   - Disadvantage: can take a long time

As you can see, each way has its own advantages and disadvantages. My opinion is that the third way, in which a decision is made by consensus, is probably generally the best as it is most likely to lead to colleagues' commitment to the decision and its implementation.

In particular, a decision that is discussed and arrived at by a group has distinct advantages over a decision made by one individual, for the following reasons.

● Each of us has our own weaknesses, activities or areas of thinking that we consider particularly important ('hobbyhorses') or particularly unimportant ('blind spots'). It takes a group to balance out and widen our own perspective.
● The decision itself will need to be implemented by other people and the more they have been involved in making the decision as well as agreeing with it, the more likely they are to be fully committed to it and support its implementation to others.

**TIP** *Try to reach a collective decision: at least if the decision is wrong, blame will come to the whole group and not just one person. If necessary, discuss a delicate issue with a colleague in private rather than in a group, as 'political' matters may come into play in the wider group.*

## Acknowledge your weaknesses ... and your strengths

Now is a good opportunity to emphasize the point just made. Each one of us has our weaknesses and strengths. While we all want to emphasize our strengths, which we consider particularly important and will mention whenever we can, we often ignore the things about ourselves that we don't consider particularly important because they are in fact weaknesses and we want to avoid doing things that we find difficult or unpleasant.

Are you aware of your own weaknesses and strengths? Think back to school reports or ask friends – some aspects may be obvious to them but not to you!

My own weaknesses are:

● lack of creativity
● being too organized

● being poor at physical activity, e.g. sports and DIY around the house.

My strengths are:

● the ability to listen
● the ability to ask insightful questions
● my (usually!) personable nature
● being methodical.

Notice that a strength can also be a weakness: one of my strengths (being methodical) is also one of my weaknesses (being too organized). I expect everyone around me (colleagues, friends and family members) to be as organized and methodical as I am and I have learned (or, more correctly, am still learning!) not to be too disappointed when they are not.

Because we each have different weaknesses and strengths, we need to balance them out with the different qualities that other colleagues possess to be able to make balanced decisions. This means that a team ideally needs a range of types of people who can take on different roles.

# Team roles

The members of a team should together bring a valuable and wide range of roles. These different roles complement one another: one person's weakness is balanced out by another person's strengths. What are the different roles?

A widely known set of different roles was developed by Dr Meredith Belbin as he looked at how members of teams behaved. He distinguishes nine different team roles, as shown in the following table.

This analysis is useful since it can reveal that there may be gaps in your team. If you find that your team is lacking certain skills, you can then actively seek to cover them.

 **TIP** *For more information about teams and how to identify colleagues' different roles, see www.belbin.com*

| Role | Qualities |
|---|---|
| Plant | Creative; good at coming up with fresh ideas and solving difficult problems in unconventional ways |
| Resource investigator | Outgoing; good at communicating with outside agencies and finding opportunities and information |
| Co-ordinator | Good as chairperson, focusing team members on the goals; a good delegator |
| Shaper | Dynamic action person who can lead and drive a project forward through difficulties |
| Monitor/evaluator | Able to stand back and bring objective discernment to evaluate different options |
| Team worker | Bringing harmony and diplomacy for good team spirit |
| Implementer (company worker) | Dependable, efficient, practical organizer who knows the company or organization well |
| Completer/finisher | Able to follow through meticulously on details to complete a project |
| Specialist | Giving expert technical knowledge |

## Teambuilding in action

I led an awayday for a group I'm connected with, as we were beginning to work together as a team. Using the Belbin model, I ended up (re-)discovering that I had skills in co-ordinating/chairing, so I was formally asked to chair meetings. Some people offered more than one role: for example, our resource investigator, who is good at communicating with many outside contacts, is also an excellent team worker who brings tact and a good spirit to team meetings. A discussion between our team members then revealed that we had no monitor/evaluator, one who could stand back and objectively assess ideas. Identifying someone with those skills was therefore one of our aims.

As well as the different roles that people play, team members should be just that: team members who are willing to work alongside others. The term *synergy* is often used to describe what happens in a successful team. It is often defined as 2 + 2 = 5, meaning that when two groups of two people work together, the result is greater than simply the sum of their individual skills. Something extra happens: the combined effect is greater.

A simpler concept was developed by Robert Dilts, known for his work in neurolinguistic programming (NLP). He distinguishes three team roles:

1 **dreamer:** a visionary with creative ideas
2 **realist:** a colleague who puts the ideas into practice and makes them happen
3 **critic:** a colleague who gives constructive criticism as he/she tests and evaluates the thoughts of the dreamer and the realist.

Whichever model you adopt or adapt, they both show that you need a range of abilities and skills in your decision-making group in order for it to be able to make balanced decisions.

## Not everyone needs to be involved in every decision

Despite the importance of having a range of different people in a decision-making group, not everyone needs to be involved in every decision.

The so-called RACI analysis helps distinguish certain colleagues:

- **R** – colleagues, e.g. directors and executives, who are **responsible** for making a decision
- **A** – colleagues, e.g. directors, who are ultimately **accountable** for a decision
- **C** – colleagues, e.g. consultants or experts, or suppliers or trades unions, who are **consulted** about decisions but who do not actually make the decisions themselves
- **I** – colleagues, e.g. assistants, who are **informed** about decisions that have been made but who need not be consulted.

# The importance of meetings

The meeting is the forum at which decisions are made, so we need to be clear about:

- the purpose of meetings
- preparing for meetings
- participating in meetings
- follow-up from meetings.

## The purpose of meetings

Meetings are useful to:

- inform colleagues, e.g. to introduce new goals or give an update on progress
- discuss with colleagues, e.g. plan together the way ahead or evaluate different options to solve a problem
- reach a decision and agree the next steps to be taken to implement the decision
- develop a sense of identity as members interact with one another and as you motivate your team.

## Preparing for meetings

The key to a successful meeting lies in the preparation and the following preparation is essential.

- **Know the purpose of the meeting.**
- **Plan a venue and time** (start and finish) in advance.
- **Invite the key people** to participate in advance.
- **Circulate an agenda in advance.** This means that you will have thought about the structure and purpose of the meeting beforehand. Also, circulate important papers with the agenda, not at the meeting itself. Ideally, the length of such papers should be no more than one page each.
- **Prepare the meeting room.** Plan the seating: chairs around a table invite discussion.
- **Read reports in advance.** If reports have been circulated before a meeting, then read them. I have been in too many meetings where we have sat during the meeting reading material that should have been read in advance.

- **Ensure that you come with accurate information.** If the meeting is to monitor progress, for example, make sure you take all your latest data on progress with you.

## The role of the chair

A good chair is a diplomatic and organized leader, someone whom the colleagues trust and someone who values, motivates and involves others, checking that they understand the points discussed. Ideally, he or she will be able to quieten down those who talk too much and also draw out those who talk too little but who can still make valuable contributions. The chair will state the key aims and objectives of items being discussed, summarize progress and bring together the points raised, to reach agreement and draw conclusions. If a point has been controversial, the chair can express exactly what is to be minuted, to avoid possible misinterpretation later. A good chair will also sense when the time is right to bring a discussion to an end and be able to come to clear decisions.

### Rescuing a failing project

Imran was called in to troubleshoot on a failing project. The existing project manager was beginning not to cope with the growing responsibilities of the project. Fortunately, Imran had a good working relationship with him.

Imran quickly noticed that basic points were missing: meetings were poorly structured with the barest agenda. During the meetings, discussions rambled on for a long time, often without decisions being made. Even when key action points were agreed, they were not noted, followed through or even reviewed at the next meeting. No wonder the project was in a mess!

As Imran had good relationships with all the colleagues, he was quickly able to put in place well-structured meetings that he chaired effectively with good decision-making skills, action points and reviews at the next meeting, so the project got back on track.

**TIP** *The key to a successful meeting lies in the preparation.*

## Presenting an argument in a meeting

When presenting an argument in a meeting, it is essential to bear in mind the following dos and don'ts.

**Do:**

- present facts clearly
- put forward arguments logically
- support your arguments with relevant quotations, easily comprehensible facts and examples (case studies)
- give reasons for and against a course of action
- keep to the main point at issue
- challenge yourself and others, and question assumptions
- play the 'devil's advocate' – put forward an argument that is completely different from your own to test the strength of your own argument

**Don't:**

- think of plausible but untrue reasons to justify a course of action
- just guess; always give reasons for your choices
- only think of reasons that support the option you want to choose
- give in to peer pressure to conform to everyone else's opinion. Stand up for what you believe is right and express your own opinion. (A committee should not simply consist of people who will always unquestioningly agree with the chair's opinions.)
- disagree with someone else's opinion in an awkward or nasty way, but show respect for others.

## Participating in meetings

Everyone has a part to play in a successful meeting. I have never understood how people can come out of a meeting asking, 'What was the point of that?' when they themselves have not contributed anything. Each of us needs to contribute in the following ways.

- **Listen well and concentrate.**
  Switch phones off and don't read or send emails or text messages; and don't interrupt when someone else is talking.
- **Ask for clarification.**
  If you are unsure about a point that has been made, it's highly likely that other colleagues will also want clarification but have been afraid to ask, for fear of looking ignorant.
- **Be constructive and have a positive attitude.**
  Even if you disagree with what has been said, there are respectful ways of expressing a difference of opinion by challenging an idea without angrily criticizing a person expressing the idea or publicly blaming an individual for a wrong action.

- **Confront the issues.**
  Focus on the real issues; don't get sidetracked.
- **Be willing to change your mind.**
  If you are listening and persuasive arguments have been offered, allow yourself to be convinced by them and change your opinion about an issue.

# Negotiating: win–win situations

In negotiating, we are aiming for a win–win situation. A win–win situation can perhaps be well illustrated by an example. My son Ben has just moved to Asia and he wanted to sell his camera. His friend Rob wanted a camera to take photographs on his travels. Ben sold Rob his camera, so both won: they each gained what they wanted – Ben money, Rob a camera.

In his book *The 7 Habits of Highly Effective People, Personal Workbook* (Simon & Schuster, 2005), Stephen Covey points out that the basics of a win–win situation are in our character. If we have the courage of our convictions but not much consideration for others, we will think win–lose. If we are too considerate but lack courage to express our views, we will think lose–win. We need a balance of both courage and consideration for win–win.

## A good negotiator of contracts

Danielle was respected as a good negotiator of contracts. The secret of her success lay in good planning. She spent a long time thinking through different business models and pricing levels so that, when it came to the negotiations, she knew exactly what approach to take. After both sides had presented their initial case, she was sometimes able to detect the weak points in the arguments of the other side and exploit them according to her own personality.

When they came to the final bargaining, she had clarified the critical issue (the price) in her mind and knew that she could be flexible on the less significant matters – for example, she didn't mind bringing delivery of the products forward by six weeks. She was assertive and firm on what was non-negotiable, however: the price. So she was able to settle and close deals well and arrange the next steps in the business relationship between the two sides.

# SMART decisions

At a meeting it is vital to ensure that action points are clear, and in particular who is responsible for following up the specific points and by when. The action points should be SMART, as shown in the following table.

| Letter | Meaning | Example |
|---|---|---|
| S | Specific, not vague | Not: 'We want to increase profits', but 'We want to increase profits by £100,000.' |
| M | Measurable and quantifiable | You have included milestones along the way to assess progress. |
| A | Agreed | All present at the meeting are in accord with next steps. |
| R | Realistic/ Resourced | 'If you want me to complete this task, you need to provide me with the resources to enable me to do so.' |
| T | Timed | What date are actions to be completed by? |
| Some colleagues also add –ER to give SMARTER: | | |
| E | Evaluated | At a later meeting, progress is assessed. |
| R | Reported | The evaluation is recorded at the next meeting. |

# Follow-up from meetings

A meeting where decisions are made but no one acts on these decisions is a waste of time. If colleagues have action points to pursue, those colleagues should follow them up.

The minutes of a meeting are a record of what happened in a meeting, including its action points. The person taking the minutes does not need to write down everything that goes on, but significant decisions, especially the action points concerning dates, schedules and financial matters, must be noted specifically.

The sooner the minutes of a meeting are circulated to those present at the meeting and other key colleagues, the more likely it is that colleagues will follow up the action points asked of them. A good manager will also follow through between meetings on the progress of the key action items; he or she will not leave it to the next meeting only to discover that action has not been taken and that valuable time has been lost.

# Summary

Today we asked the question, 'Who makes decisions in your company or organization?' and considered teams making decisions, team roles and the importance of meetings.

## Follow-up

Think of a major decision that your company or organization has made recently.

1 How much were colleagues involved in the decision-making process? What was the relationship between their involvement and their motivation to implement the decision?

2 List three strengths and three weaknesses that you have. Check your responses with colleagues and/or friends.

3 Look at your answer to 2. How many of your weaknesses are balanced out by the strengths of other members of your team?

4 Think about the meetings you hold. How could you make them more effective? Be as practical as possible.

5 Consider the actions of the last meeting you attended. Were they SMART? If not, what will you do about it?

SUNDAY  MONDAY  TUESDAY  WEDNESDAY  THURSDAY  FRIDAY  SATURDAY

# Fact-check [answers at the back]

1. As team leader, why should you share the decision-making process with others?
   a) To avoid taking full responsibility ❑
   b) To compensate for my own insecurity ❑
   c) To increase their motivation ❑
   d) To increase their pay ❑

2. What does 'consensus' mean?
   a) Counting how many people are present ❑
   b) General agreement by people ❑
   c) Agreeing to have different views ❑
   d) Many people waiting for a bus ❑

3. What should an effective team consist of?
   a) All similar kinds of people so that decisions are made as slowly as possible ❑
   b) A group so large that you don't know everyone's name ❑
   c) All similar kinds of people so that decisions are made as quickly as possible ❑
   d) A range of different kinds of people so that different approaches can be considered ❑

4. What is synergy?
   a) The result of people working together being more successful than when they each work separately ❑
   b) The result of people working separately being more effective than when they work together ❑
   c) Energy produced by all the colleagues in the room ❑
   d) The wrong things colleagues have done in the past ❑

5. What does RACI stand for?
   a) Relationships, accountability, consultation, intention ❑
   b) Resources, assessments, choice, implementation ❑
   c) Respect, authority, competition, integrity ❑
   d) Responsible, accountable, consulted, informed ❑

6. What is the key to a successful meeting?
   a) The refreshments ❑
   b) The room ❑
   c) The length of time it lasts ❑
   d) The preparation ❑

7. How should you put forward
   an argument?
   a) Present only the advantages
      of each of the options ❏
   b) Present the advantages and
      disadvantages of each of the
      options ❏
   c) Don't bother with advantages
      or disadvantages ❏
   d) Present only the
      disadvantages of all the
      options I discount ❏

8. What attitude should you
   show if you disagree with
   the boss?
   a) Respect ❏
   b) Humour ❏
   c) Sarcasm ❏
   d) Awkwardness ❏

9. What does the acronym
   SMART stand for?
   a) Schedules, markets,
      assumptions, recruitment/
      risk, trends ❏
   b) Strategy, marketing, assets,
      regulation/resources,
      trust ❏
   c) Specific, measurable, agreed,
      realistic/resourced, timed ❏
   d) Shareholders, management,
      authority, respect/roles,
      training ❏

10. As a manager chairing a
    meeting, what should you
    seek to do?
    a) Pay more attention to the
       colleagues I like ❏
    b) Involve all the colleagues
       on my team ❏
    c) Wander from the subject as
       much as possible to avoid
       taking a decision ❏
    d) Ignore everyone else and
       talk all the time ❏

# THURSDAY

# Evaluate different options

You now know your aims and have collected relevant information and identified different options. Working effectively in a team, your next task is to evaluate these different options so that you can come to a decision.

Your aim here is to reduce the number of options available, to enable you to make the right decision. It is sometimes easier to say that you don't want to choose a particular option (and why you don't want to) than to say what you do want.

Today we will look at:

- distinguishing different aspects of the decision
- setting objective criteria against which you can then assess each of your different options
- considering the consequences of each option
- listing the advantages and disadvantages and/or essential and desirable qualities of each option
- the need to compromise: probably no option is perfect
- costing the different options open to you
- assessing risks: knowing how and when things could go wrong and therefore being prepared for them.

# Distinguish different aspects of the decision

Many people have found Edward de Bono's 'six thinking hats' helpful. He distinguishes:

- **the white hat:** an analytical and objective consideration of facts and information
- **the red hat:** looking at a subject from an emotional point of view. What do colleagues feel about it?
- **the black hat:** looking at a subject from a critical point of view, considering its negative aspects, risks and disadvantages. What is the worst possible scenario?
- **the yellow hat:** looking at a subject from a positive, optimistic and visionary viewpoint, considering its advantages
- **the green hat:** looking at a subject from a creative viewpoint, examining any fresh constructive ideas
- **the blue hat:** looking at a subject in a structured way and coming to a decision.

Applying 'the six hats' means that you value different thoughts but you can separate objective facts from subjective feelings, advantages from disadvantages, and creative from structured viewpoints. We will now examine these different ways of evaluating options in the decision-making process.

# Set objective criteria

This is the 'white hat' way of thinking. Years ago, my wife and I needed to buy a new house. We had one child and wanted a larger family. I needed office space: working from the dining-room table was all right in the short term but not suitable for the long run. We drew up a shortlist of the criteria we wanted for a house:

1 at least three bedrooms
2 at least two rooms downstairs, one of which could be used as an office
3 a more modern house than our current one (built in 1901)

4 within walking distance of the town centre (at that time my wife couldn't drive)

5 within our price range.

Eventually we settled on one that fulfilled all the criteria. The first two criteria were relatively easy to fulfil – most of the houses we looked at matched these. (In fact, the house we bought had only one large room downstairs but we converted the integral garage into an office.) Number 4 was the critical one – the new house had to be within 15 minutes or so of the town centre – and to achieve it we had to ignore some of the nicer houses in category 5.

What were the steps we took in this part of the decision-making process?

1 We analysed the situation.
2 We established certain objective criteria.
3 We looked at a wide range of options (houses) to see which fulfilled our criteria.
4 We narrowed down the choice to two or three houses that satisfied our criteria.

Using our criteria, we were able to reject perhaps 90 per cent of the properties for which we received details without needing to view them. Many houses were possible, but far fewer were realistic, for the reasons we had identified – as old as our previous house; too far away from the town centre; too expensive – so we quickly eliminated those from our thinking.

**When examining different options, eliminate those that are possible but unrealistic.**

Alongside these steps we also used 'red hat' thinking, the intuitive sense of 'Yes, we can live in this house,' that we felt on viewing the house we eventually chose. Look back at Tuesday for more on intuition.

> When I go to a restaurant, sometimes I find it easy to know which dish to choose: an Indian curry! If no Indian curries are on the menu, I set some criteria and go through the choices, eliminating the dishes I don't want and then settling for the one I don't want least.

# Distinguish essential and desirable qualities

When setting criteria to inform your decision, you will need to distinguish between those that are essential and those that are desirable. For example, when recruiting new staff, you will need to define the skills, qualifications and experience that the person you are looking for will have. You do this in a **person specification**. Some of these qualities will be essential, others desirable.

For example, previous experience of a similar role is usually considered essential: to be a team leader of staff at a customer services help desk, for instance, it is essential that the person has previous experience of working in customer services. Depending on the position you want to fill, you might be looking for a good team player or for a 'lone ranger' who is better at working by themselves, for someone who can plan ahead or someone who works well with spreadsheets. Some of these qualities may be desirable rather than essential.

You can list the fulfilling of criteria objectively by setting up a chart like this one for prospective candidates.

| | Previous experience in customer services? | Team player (T) or lone ranger (L)? | Organized |
|---|---|---|---|
| Jo | No | T | Yes |
| Louise | Yes | T | Yes |
| Henry | Yes | L | ? |

Using these criteria, you offer Louise the job because she has previous experience in customer services, is a good team player and is organized.

If the choice within each category is not a definite yes or no, you can give a numerical value to each, e.g. on a scale of 1 to 5, with minus numbers indicating disadvantages (– 5 most disadvantageous) and plus numbers indicating advantages (+ 5 most advantageous). You can then add up the scores to see which option will be more advantageous overall, as in the following example.

| | Previous experience in customer services? | Team player (+) or lone ranger (-) | Organized | Total |
|---|---|---|---|---|
| Jo | – 1 | + 3 | + 4 | 6 |
| Louise | + 4 | + 5 | + 5 | 14 |
| Henry | + 3 | – 3 | + 1 | 1 |

Such a numerical analysis highlights even more strongly that Louise is the best candidate.

# Consider the consequences

Every decision has consequences, and your task as manager is to:

● be aware of the risks of choosing different options
● evaluate the risks of choosing different options
● minimize the risks of choosing different options.

To do this, you need to do more than imagine you *might* choose a particular option: you need to think about what would happen if you *did* choose it. Be both subjective (e.g. what would it feel like?) and objective (e.g. what would be the profit or loss?).

Use criteria that are in line with the values that you and/or your company or organization hold. It would feel nice to have £1,000,000, but the only way of getting that much money – by robbing a bank – does not align with my values!

Here, you deliberately think of some 'what ifs'.

● What would happen if you did nothing? Sometimes this is a valid option. Sometimes – but not always – the response to a crisis can be to continue as if nothing has happened because the crisis will exhaust itself and fade away.

● What would happen if the decision were not made now? Can you delay it?

● What would happen if the decision were not made by you? Is it your decision to make – or is it the responsibility of you and others? (See also Wednesday.)

● What would happen if you adopted each one of the options that emerge? You need to think about this before you make your choice. For example, when preparing for negotiations, consider whether agreeing to deliver the products within three months is a realistic schedule for you. If it is not, don't offer it in the first place.

● What possible future situations could develop?

## Avoiding adverse consequences

Max was great at his engineering job. His technical knowledge of the company's products was outstanding. He knew the background to each kind of wheel and all the different specifications and measurements for each nut and bolt. However, he was poor at building good working relationships. No one was quite sure how he came to be shortlisted in the interviews for a new sales rep for the company.

Fortunately, the sales director who interviewed him realized that he would be a disastrous choice, and a colleague with slightly less technical knowledge but far better people skills was appointed. The sales director had considered the adverse consequences of appointing Max to be their new sales rep.

**TIP** *When considering the consequences of a decision, imagine yourself in the situation, experiment and then consider the advantages and disadvantages of each option. In this way you are more likely to avoid adverse consequences.*

# List the advantages and disadvantages

Weighing up different options by considering their advantages and disadvantages is best illustrated by an example, as follows.

| Disadvantages of keeping old computer system | Advantages of installing new computer system A | Advantages of installing new computer system B |
|---|---|---|
| The existing system: <br> ● keeps breaking down <br> ● is too complex to handle present needs <br> ● is not compatible with the department's processes <br> ● cannot handle the production of reports that Head Office now demands. | This new system: <br> ● is compatible with most other departments' systems <br> ● can handle the production of reports that Head Office now demands <br> ● will save time in that it is far easier to operate than the existing system. | This new system: <br> ● is compatible with only one department's systems <br> ● cannot handle the production of reports that Head Office now demands <br> ● will save time in that it is far easier to operate than the existing system <br> ● is half the price of system A. |

The conclusions you might draw from the example include the following.

- It is possible that we could keep the existing system but it is inefficient.
- While the initial costs of installing a new computer system are high, the benefits to the company in time saved will come within a few months of installation.
- System A is more expensive than B but A can do more of what we need so, although the initial cost is higher, it will save time and therefore money in the medium term.

## Realize the need to compromise

As you weigh up the various alternatives before you, you will probably need to compromise. We need to realize that we do not live in an ideal world and therefore no one option is likely to fulfil all the essential and desirable features. For example, you may be running late on a project and have to outsource a particular part of it. You find suitable colleagues who can undertake that part of the project well, but the disadvantage is the cost of paying such staff, which significantly exceeds your budget. Nonetheless, you decide to go ahead and outsource that part of the project because you consider that the advantage – that the project will be delivered on time and you will retain your client – far outweighs the disadvantage of the higher bill. (You learn from your mistake, and next time you will be better at planning both the schedules and the costs.)

The term *trade-off* is used to refer to a compromise: you obtain an advantage but have to make some sacrifice, as with the trade-off between individual freedom and public security.

# Cost your different options

Think about the resources you need to fulfil each of your different options. There are four different aspects to consider.

1 **Budget** – prepare a budget for each option and see which produces the greatest profit (or the lowest loss). Look back at Monday on preparing a budget.

2 **ROI** – calculate the return on investment and consider which option produces the greatest (see Monday).

3 **Risks** – calculate the costs of dealing with possible risks (see later today).

4 **Business category** – consider which category the aspect of business falls into according to 'the growth–share matrix' developed by the Boston Consulting Group (BCG) in the 1970s.

The BCG's founder Bruce Henderson observed that a company's business units or products could be considered as belonging to one of four categories. The categories are based on relative market share and market growth.

### ● Cash cows

These are products that generate high income relative to the low cost of retaining their large market share. Such products are 'milked' – producing profits easily and continuously.

### ● Dogs

These products have a low market share and a low rate of growth. They remain in production mainly for sentimental reasons, but they are not profitable and are therefore likely to be sold off.

- **Question marks** (also called **problem children** or **wildcats**)
  These products have a low market share but a high rate of growth. Their future profitability is uncertain but they might become stars.
- **Stars**
  These are profitable products with a high market share and a high rate of growth, and they are likely to be invested in strongly.

The Boston growth–share matrix

| | Relative market share: high | Relative market share: low |
|---|---|---|
| Market growth: high | Stars | Question marks |
| Market growth: low | Cash cows | Dogs |

## It's not just about cost

For a forthcoming business trip to Germany, do I choose a more expensive international hotel or a cheaper local one? I have found a good local one on the Internet, but it does not provide evening meals, which of course the international one does. However, thinking about it, I've realized that I will not want an evening meal except for on the first evening, as I may well have a good lunch in the restaurant at the university where I will be lecturing. Perhaps my lurking fear is that I will be stranded and starving on a Sunday evening in a large German city – hardly realistic!

The lessons I am learning are to explore every option in detail so that I am as fully informed as possible about the decision I am making. Cost may not be the most significant factor.

# Assess the risks of each option

Risk assessment is **knowing how and when things could go wrong and dealing with them**. It is important to manage risks so that the threats of possible risks are minimized. For example, if you are making decisions about managing a project, risks are the uncertain events that could happen which could prevent your project from being carried out successfully.

Questions to ask yourself might include the following.

- Is the schedule realistic?
- Have sufficient financial resources been made available?
- Are roles and responsibilities clear?
- Are you measuring the quality of what you are producing objectively enough?

Risks need to be identified, assessed and then dealt with. The one key point to remember is that you will not survive in business without encountering certain risks, so it is better to plan to deal with them than be surprised when they unexpectedly arise.

You should prepare a risk-assessment document that lists potential risks, their probability of occurrence, the extent of their effect on your project objectives and your responses to them. The following example shows a risk assessment for a holiday booking company.

| Risk | Probability | Effect | Response |
|------|-------------|--------|----------|
| Publicity inadequate | Low | Medium | Revise publicity; go to a new supplier |
| Computer software breaks down | Medium | High | Ensure technicians are available 24/7 |
| Too many bookings | Medium | High | Identify other accommodation |
| Poor weather | Medium | High | Include holidays with indoor activities |

You could even add a further column to indicate the likely cost of implementing the response. Here, do not pluck figures out of the air, but undertake research to ensure that they are fair estimates.

When it comes to decision making, you need to act at least on those options that have a medium probability. Time spent preparing for unforeseen events is not wasted: if they should occur, you will be ready.

*'Hope for the best; plan for the worst.'*

Anon.

# Summary

Today we've looked at evaluating different options, weighing up your choices by distinguishing different aspects of the decision-making process (de Bono's six thinking hats). We have looked at setting objective criteria, considering the consequences, listing advantages and disadvantages and distinguishing essential and desirable qualities. We also explained the importance of compromise. Finally, we looked at ways of costing options and assessing risks.

### Follow-up

Take Edward de Bono's six thinking hats and apply them to a decision you need to make.

1 The white hat: what are the objective facts?

2 The red hat: what do colleagues feel about the issues?

3 The black hat: what disadvantages do the various options have?

4 The yellow hat: what advantages and benefits do the various options bring?

5 The green hat: what fresh creative alternatives and ideas can you think of?

6 The blue hat: where are you up to in the structure of making the decision?

SUNDAY MONDAY TUESDAY WEDNESDAY THURSDAY FRIDAY SATURDAY

# Fact-check [answers at the back]

1. When evaluating different options, what should your aim be?
   a) To draw pretty pictures ❑
   b) To increase the number of options available ❑
   c) To draw complex charts ❑
   d) To reduce the number of options available ❑

2. In de Bono's 'six thinking hats', what do the white and red hats represent?
   a) The white hat represents facts and the red hat feelings ❑
   b) The white hat represents feelings and the red hat facts ❑
   c) The white hat represents purity and the red hat love ❑
   d) The white hat represents light and the red hat joy ❑

3. What criteria should you use when evaluating options?
   a) Subjective ❑
   b) Objective ❑
   c) What are 'criteria'? ❑
   d) Different ones, depending on the options ❑

4. How often should you consider the advantages and disadvantages of different options?
   a) Occasionally ❑
   b) Never ❑
   c) Always ❑
   d) When I feel like it ❑

5. When drafting a person specification, what should you distinguish?
   a) Subjective and objective qualities ❑
   b) Essential and desirable qualities ❑
   c) Whether I like the person or not ❑
   d) Management and leadership qualities ❑

6. How should you consider the consequences of each option?
   a) Informally in my mind ❑
   b) As if they actually happened ❑
   c) Never ❑
   d) In so much detail that I never make a decision ❑

7. What does trade-off mean?
   a) A business that is sold ❑
   b) A compromise: you obtain an advantage but have to make some sacrifice ❑
   c) The profit you gain from selling a product ❑
   d) An arrangement in which you give a used article (e.g. an old car) as part payment for a new product (e.g. a new car) ❑

8. What are cash cows?
a) Milk, cheese and other dairy products for sale at a supermarket ❏
b) Products that generate high income relative to the low cost of retaining their large market share ❏
c) Products with a low market share and low market growth ❏
d) Products with a high market share and high market growth ❏

9. How should you cost different options?
a) As infrequently as possible ❏
b) I don't; I hope for the best ❏
c) Objectively and methodically ❏
d) Imaginatively, by plucking figures out of the air ❏

10. What is a risk?
a) An event that will definitely happen and have a good effect on your decision ❏
b) An uncertain event that could affect the success of an option ❏
c) An event that will definitely happen and have a bad effect on your decision ❏
d) A game you play ❏

**FRIDAY**

# Make an informed decision

Now you're finally at the point of coming to a decision. You know the core issues, you've gathered information, and you've identified and evaluated the various options. You're about to make the decision. How do you feel? Are you still uncertain or do you now consider yourself to be in control of the situation?

We will look at the emotions you may experience as you draw closer to the point of making your decision and also at how you feel after having made the decision.

We will also consider:

- arriving at the actual decision
- implementing your decision: the next steps
- communicating your decision
- planning for change.

We will see that, after the decision has been made, you will need leadership qualities and interpersonal skills to implement it, especially in communicating it and working through both the 'big picture' and the details.

# Factors against making a decision

Many factors may stand in the way of you making your final decision.

- **Do you feel confused?**
  You may have too much information even after evaluating all the options. Look back at Tuesday on moving beyond confusion.
- **Do you want to continue to analyse the issues,** identifying and evaluating future options?
  Act; don't over-analyse. By temperament, I'm an analyser. Fortunately, my wife is an action person – that's why we make a good team. At the end of the day, you need to stop analysing and make a decision.
- **Do you think that you still do not have enough information?**
  Often, you will have to make decisions without knowing the full picture. Recently, on one of my courses, a colleague was being asked to make decisions but it was as if she was being asked to assemble a jigsaw of which not only the picture was lost but also half the pieces were missing.

- **Do you feel too tense to make a decision?**
  In this case, try trusted ways to relax and/or seek the advice of trusted colleagues or friends. When my mother died suddenly and unexpectedly just after the 9/11 terrorist attacks in 2001, she was on holiday in Australia and the rest of the family was in the UK. In the immediate aftermath of 9/11, it seemed unclear whether insurers were insuring

planes to fly. As a family, we had to decide which of us three children in the UK (plus spouses), if any, would fly out. It was a hard decision to make, but close friends were very helpful at this point: 'You must go,' my friend Michael told me. It would after all have been unthinkable for me not to attend my own mother's funeral, so I went. Friends pushed me to go when I was unable to make the decision for myself.

● **Do you feel afraid of making the wrong decision?**
What if you choose that option and it fails? If you're afraid of making mistakes, you may well end up doing nothing. Remember, the person who never made mistakes never made anything. The key is to learn from your mistakes.

> **'The person who never made mistakes never made anything.'**
>
> Theodore Roosevelt, US president (1858–1919)

# Arriving at a decision

The moment has come to make the decision. But what does that mean? In many situations, the best decision will often emerge as you weigh up the various options. As you go through the stages that lead up to reaching the decision, an option may well just feel right: you have identified and evaluated the various options open to you and you choose the one that seems objectively right.

What then? What do you do after making the decision?

# Implement your decision: the next steps

I remember it well. My colleague and I had taken our proposal to Penguin Books, and they had decided to publish our dictionary (as referred to on Tuesday). I got the phone call saying, 'Yes!' But I wasn't prepared, and I didn't know what to do next. This was because I hadn't planned it. Fortunately, I lost only a few hours' worth of work and I used those hours to think and work out the next steps that I had to pursue.

There are always things to do to implement a decision, such as:

- sign contracts, legal papers or other documents
- make phone calls to inform relevant people of the decision
- compose emails and letters that confirm in writing precisely what you are committing yourself to
- arrange to see people (perhaps phoning them first and then following up with an email)
- plan later stages, which might include:
  - establishing priorities and a list of tasks: draw up a spreadsheet or Gantt chart to show the tasks, schedules and personnel responsible for different tasks
  - planning the overall view: set out the milestones of progress to be fulfilled within the overall task
  - planning the detail of each stage: list the order in which certain items need to be undertaken
  - integrating your decision into your normal cycle of planning: for example, if you are increasing your mortgage, add that to your list of bank standing orders.

Be realistic. As the proverb puts it, 'Rome wasn't built in a day.' It takes a long time and much effort to achieve great things and you will need patience and perseverance to see the whole decision implemented.

Be courageous. As a manager, you are called on to provide leadership. You are the captain of the ship: you need to face up to the challenges, have the courage of your convictions and pursue what you know to be the right course of action. I used to think that courage is the opposite of fear, but it isn't: courage is an inner strength to decide to do something difficult or dangerous, even if the fears are present: 'Feel the fear and do it anyway.'

> *'Each indecision brings its own delays and days are lost lamenting over lost days ... What you can do or think you can do, begin it. For boldness has magic, power and genius in it.'*
>
> Johann Wolfgang Von Goethe, German poet, scientist and writer (1749–1832)

---

**The point of no return**

The point of no return is the moment in a journey or project at which the person has to continue: it is now too late to turn back or reverse the decision.

---

# Communicate your decision

Among the next steps we need to take, outlined above, one of the most important is to consider the 'people' aspect of the decision and how you will communicate your decision to them. You will need to decide (!) exactly what to communicate and what you want to achieve. This means communicating not just that the decision has been made (the 'big picture') but also what this means for individual members of staff and others involved (the detail). For example, 'Good news! We've just won a major contract to supply ... with ... and that means the further project will provide work for us through to the end of next year. Over the next few days, we'll let you know what this means for all the different teams.'

It will be important to clarify roles and responsibilities and make sure that colleagues have the resources they need to fulfil the agreed tasks. Such an approach will help secure buy-in from a wide circle of colleagues.

Take into account the following.

1 Think *who* the best person is to communicate the decision. This may not be the same person as the one who made the decision. Who is best at communicating with colleagues? If the news is bad, who has developed the most trusted working relationships and would be best suited to breaking such news?

2 Think *how* to communicate the decision.
Should this be face to face or by email or by phone? Email is not good for every form of business communication, particularly if the matter is delicate (see below), when face to face is better.

3 Explain not only *what* you are doing but also *why* you are doing it. This is especially important when communicating an unwelcome change, for example, 'Profits are down, so we need to re-assign certain members of staff to different areas of work.'

## Dealing with a sensitive matter

If the matter is sensitive, always seek a personal meeting, rather than communicating your decision by text, email or phone or in public.

- Where possible, alert the person to whom you have to make known the decision in advance. This can be done subtly – 'I've been wondering about ...' – or more explicitly: 'Could we have a chat about ...'
- Prepare for the meeting, both what you will say and how you will respond to the other person's potential reactions.

- At the personal meeting, be clear and honest, affirming your respect for the other person.
- Listen to the other person's response: seek to understand their interests as well as your own.
- Seek to end the meeting on a positive note.

## Resolving conflict

At times you are bound to meet conflict. Seek to deal with conflict quickly by tackling the issues. Don't be cautious and fearful about speaking directly and clearly about difficulties.

Two useful books on the subject of conflict resolution are:

- Douglas Stone et al., *Difficult conversations: How to Discuss What Matters Most* (Michael Joseph, 1999)
- Ken Sande, *The Peacemaker: A Biblical Guide to Resolving Personal Conflict* (Baker, 1991).

The following is based on what those authors helpfully suggest.

1 Distinguish the incident – what is happening/happened – from feelings about the incident. Consider separately the following:
   - the incident – someone said something; someone is to blame. Try to focus on the real issue. Remain calm. Listen closely. Ask open questions. Understand other people's interests as well as your own.
   - feelings about the incident – these may include anger or hurt.
   - the identity of the person – sometimes a person's identity, including their own self-worth, will feel threatened, so calmly affirm your respect for them.
2 Do what you can to resolve the issue and maintain the relationship:
   - prepare and evaluate possible solutions
   - agree on the way forward.

# After you have made the decision

After you have made the decision, how do you feel? Do you have niggling doubts as to whether you have made the right decision? In marketing terms, this feeling is known as 'buyer's remorse'. How do you deal with such feelings?

1 Know yourself. If you know you are likely to have such feelings, then accept them when they come.
2 Realize that the feelings will probably go away as you get used to the changes that the decision brings.
3 Go through in your mind all the objective steps that you have taken to reach the decision. Repeat to yourself the various steps you followed: for example, you examined the different options open to you and considered the consequences of choosing each one and their advantages and disadvantages.
4 Look at the positive side of things.
5 Above all, follow through on your next steps to implement the decision.

# Plan for change

You have made your decision and have begun to implement it. However, the rest of the world will not remain static. Your decision may also affect other people's decisions. For example, if you start making a few people redundant, other colleagues may then start looking for other jobs. Ideally, therefore, part of your decision-making process should have considered the 'what-if' situations (see Thursday). In other words, you need to plan for changes so that you are prepared for them and not surprised when they do occur.

You will need to put in place procedures that monitor and control major items such as time and cost. If you are running a project, check constantly that:

● you are on schedule
● your costs are as planned
● the quality of what you are producing or delivering reaches the agreed standard.

If any of these is not following your original intentions, then discuss and agree with others how you will adjust matters so that you get back to making the progress you want.

Be flexible and creative in solving problems that may arise. For example, on one project I was involved with, we were running late on a delivery of books from China. The books were needed for an exhibition and there wasn't enough time to send them by ship, so we made the decision to airfreight them. The cost was greater than planned but the customer was satisfied and later came back for a repeat order, when we could work on a more realistic schedule.

## The committee's finances were in a mess

The committee's finances were in a mess and the treasurer had resigned. There was, everyone thought, just about enough money to pay the three full-time staff, but the trustees knew it would be difficult. The trustees met and called on experienced colleagues to offer their expertise. This revealed that the committee would run out of funds in a few months unless drastic action was taken.

An urgent call for financial help was issued and, fortunately, the request was heeded. The extra funds gave the trustees an opportunity to put the running of the committee on a firmer financial basis. They now put in place proper monitoring controls that measured actual income and expenditure regularly and rigorously. Permission for expenditure on items over £200 had to be specially sought. By establishing such thorough controls, the trustees were able not only to survive difficult times but also to gather sound information that they could use as a basis to make wise decisions in the future.

# Summary

Today we looked at the issues around making the actual decision. We have considered the emotional side of decision making, both before and after you have made it. We have also been concerned with implementing the decision and the need to do this carefully, planning what you want to achieve. It involves creating the schedule and milestones along the way, and knowing the costs and quality of what you are delivering.

We also discussed the need to plan how you will communicate the decision to everyone affected by it, to tell them what you will do and why you are doing it.

### Follow-up

Think of a decision you made recently.

1 How important were your emotions in the immediate steps both before and after making the decision? Discuss this with a trusted friend or colleague.

2 How good were you at communicating the decision? Again, discuss your answer with the friend or colleague.

3 How flexible are you now in adjusting to the changes required since making the decision?

SUNDAY

MONDAY

TUESDAY

WEDNESDAY

THURSDAY

FRIDAY

SATURDAY

# Fact-check [answers at the back]

1. How much information do you gather before making a decision?
   a) None ❏
   b) Enough to make an informed decision ❏
   c) So much that it's difficult to make the right decision ❏
   d) Never enough, so I never make any decisions ❏

2. When you are afraid of making the wrong decision, what should you do?
   a) Still do my best to make the right decision ❏
   b) Not make any decisions ❏
   c) Spend more time analysing all the factors again ❏
   d) Toss a coin and hope for the best ❏

3. What is the point of no return?
   a) The name of a pub down the road ❏
   b) A situation in which I have not made a return on my investment ❏
   c) The point in a project when I want to start again ❏
   d) The moment in a project at which I have to continue: it is now too late to turn back or reverse the decision ❏

4. What should you do when you have made a decision?
   a) Look again at the other options ❏
   b) Move on to the next decision ❏
   c) Carefully implement the decision ❏
   d) Sit back and do nothing ❏

5. How important is it to communicate your decision?
   a) Essential ❏
   b) A waste of time ❏
   c) A luxury ❏
   d) Nice to do if you have the time ❏

6. If a subject is sensitive or delicate, how should you discuss it?
   a) I don't discuss it; it's too sensitive ❏
   b) In public ❏
   c) In private ❏
   d) Within earshot of the department ❏

7. How should you decide how to communicate a decision?
   a) Always text the decision ❏
   b) Seek to find the best way, e.g. face to face or by email or phone ❏
   c) Never communicate anyway ❏
   d) Always use email ❏

8. Who should you communicate with about a change that affects a large number of colleagues?
a) Only close friends ❏
b) The colleagues in the office next to me ❏
c) Everyone in the company ❏
d) All those with an involvement or interest to ensure their buy-in ❏

9. How should you respond when changes occur after you have made a decision?
a) With surprise ❏
b) With resignation ❏
c) By doing nothing ❏
d) Calmly; I planned for at least some of them and so am prepared ❏

10. What should you put in place to make sure your decision is implemented well?
a) My resignation letter ❏
b) A new long-term plan ❏
c) A marketing plan ❏
d) Monitoring and control procedures ❏

SUNDAY MONDAY TUESDAY WEDNESDAY THURSDAY FRIDAY SATURDAY

# SATURDAY

## Review the decision carefully

Congratulations! You have made your decision and are putting it into action. You have worked successfully through all the different stages of the decision-making process.

Is this the end? No: now is an excellent time to review how you have managed the whole decision-making process. So today we will look at evaluating the process by going through the week's main stages:

- defining your aims clearly
- collecting the relevant information
- identifying different options
- evaluating the different options
- looking at what has gone well and also learning from your mistakes.

We will complete the week by considering the qualities of a good decision maker.

# Evaluate the decision-making process

Let's review the past week by going back through the stages of the process and checking that you have covered everything.

## Defining your aims clearly

Did you identify:

- what the real issue was that you needed to make a decision about and what the secondary issues were?
- the time when the decision had to be made by? Was that timescale realistic? If not, did you work out a strategy to seek more time?
- what kind of person you are, especially in terms of your values and what motivates you at work and the way in which you work?
- your personality regarding decision making: are you naturally decisive or indecisive, cautious or rash, for example?
- who in your company or organization makes the decisions – is it only you as manager or do you involve others?
- who will implement the decision?

what your learning style is and how this affects the way you make decisions?

*When a decision is made that affects others, the more involved the people affected are in the decision-making process the stronger their motivation will be.*

## Collecting relevant information

Regarding the decision you made, did you:

● understand the context?
● gather relevant information, including consulting experts, as necessary?
● work on your costs?

## Identifying different options

When you considered a range of techniques to help you identify different options in your decision making, did you:

● consider imaginative alternatives, widening your thinking so that you didn't stick with what you are used to and you didn't choose the first alternative that offered itself?
● challenge assumptions?
● consider where you can concentrate your resources so that they are used most effectively?
● consider the timing, working out which events come before others?

What role did intuition (your gut feelings) play?

## Evaluating the different options

Did you:

● reduce the number of options available, to enable you to make a decision?
● establish certain objective criteria against which you then assessed each of your different options?

- consider the consequences of each option and their advantages and disadvantages?
- make a compromise?
- list the resources needed to fulfil each option?
- cost the different options that were open to you?
- assess risks, knowing how and when things could go wrong and therefore being prepared for them?

## Making and implementing the decision

You eventually arrived at the point of coming to a decision. Did you:

- define the core issues?
- gather information?
- identify and evaluate the various options, weighing up each of the options in your mind and dealing with your emotions?

How are you now getting on with implementing your decision and communicating it to all the relevant colleagues? Have you set in place good monitoring controls to help you track progress?

# Learn from your mistakes

AND YOU'LL BE ABLE TO TALK TO PEOPLE HUNDREDS OF MILES AWAY.

What if you have made the wrong decision? Realize that making the wrong decision is different from having doubts when you have made the right decision (see Friday). If events have turned out completely differently from what you planned and they have become confused, complicated, or unsatisfactory compared with what you had envisaged before you made the decision, then you may need to rethink your plan.

## All was not lost

A publishing company outsourced the compilation of a new medical reference text to Harry. The project sponsor decided that Harry would be the best person to lead the project as Managing Editor, and Harry duly organized a team of consultants, compilers and subeditors for the project. Only once the project was under way did it become apparent that Harry lacked sufficient specialist medical knowledge to brief the subeditors and compilers fully. All was not lost, however. The project sponsor decided to appoint a general editor with excellent knowledge of the medical field, to work alongside Harry. Funds were agreed to finance such a role. Unfortunately, the work had to be put on hold for several months until a suitable general editor was found. However, once one was found, the project was relaunched successfully.

The result of Harry working with the general editor and all the other colleagues was an excellent reference tool. Although initially a wrong decision was made, the project sponsor used that as a basis to correct the course and turn the difficulty into a success.

Depending on the nature of the mistake, you will need to go back to the beginning again and take the following steps.

1 Plan a new series of actions that you need to undertake to reach your desired goal, using the point you have reached under the wrong decision as a basis for the new course you will now follow.
2 Deal with issues that have arisen from the wrong decision.
3 Start again.

## Reversing a decision

Organizations sometimes make a wrong decision on a grand scale. In 1985, for example, the Coca-Cola company tried to reverse the decline in its sales by reformulating the popular soft drink and launching it as 'new Coke'. The company had thought that the original Coca-Cola needed replacing to boost sales but they had underestimated the goodwill towards the brand and its iconic image in the US psyche. The launch of the new drink provoked a massive public outcry as people remembered why they loved the 'old' Coca-Cola, and new Coke was withdrawn after a mere 79 days. The company then reintroduced the original Coke, which was later rebranded as Coke Classic.

## Learn from failure

We all make mistakes in life. The other day I took my wife to a restaurant ten minutes' walk from our house. She enjoyed the meal but would have preferred to have travelled by car as her foot was painful. I made the mistake of only partly looking after her.

You may well know the story about the inventor Thomas Edison: when asked how he felt about failing to design a working light bulb, he is said to have replied, 'I have not failed. I've just found 10,000 ways that won't work.'

We often fail in life, but we can view our mistakes as opportunities to learn and become stronger people.

## Jack changed his mind

When Jack first became a manager, he found himself in charge of people who had previously been on the same level as him. Once one of them, he now was senior to them. When he became team leader, he thought he would introduce new daily briefings and new performance targets and, rather than implementing these changes gradually, he decided to introduce them all at once. He did this to try to project a confident image and to show his colleagues that he was in control.

Unfortunately, the team did not cope well with this and their attitude became negative towards him. So Jack changed his mind: he decided to try a different way. He decided to have one-to-ones with each colleague to find out their own suggestions and comments on the changes. Such sessions proved to be opportunities for them to understand that the changes were for the good of the team, and gradually Jack was able to introduce all the changes successfully.

# What makes a good decision maker?

Finally today we consider the qualities that make a good decision maker. They are:

- **integrity:** being honest and sincere; being open and transparent and not deceitful; being upright and doing what you believe to be the right thing; and dealing with all staff fairly
- **strategic thinking:** able to see the big picture and plan ahead well; proactive
- **vision:** able to see beyond the immediate situation to the ultimate goal; purposeful
- **wisdom:** having good business sense and experience
- **balance:** able to weigh up alternatives, avoiding both personal weaknesses and extravagances

- **decisiveness:** not one to put off decisions; not hesitant or dithering but firm
- **courage:** having an inner strength that can firmly face up to difficult situations, even if you are afraid
- **insight:** able to discern what is significant among complex or difficult issues
- **determination:** energetic and patient in seeing a decision through; committed and persistent to complete tasks reliably
- **creativity:** able to find fresh solutions to difficult issues; resourceful and innovative; adaptable; able to deal with people well and solve problems imaginatively
- **authority:** gaining the respect of others; influential
- **being a good motivator:** one who values, encourages and inspires others
- **diplomacy:** one who can bring together people with different opinions; able to conduct negotiations that respect others' rights; tactful; avoiding giving unnecessary offence and knowing how to deal with sensitive situations
- **being a good communicator:** able to explain a vision positively and clearly; knowing how to use words well; gracious; an encourager
- **executive ability:** good at implementing projects; good at developing others
- **being good at listening:** not too talkative but one who takes time to understand others first
- **being a good delegator:** able effectively to assign tasks to members of your team.

**TIP** *Sometimes you will not have all the facts, or your colleagues may hesitate, but you still need to have the ability to make the decision.*

# Summary

On our final day this week we have looked back at the whole of the decision-making process and tried to evaluate the different steps. How have you got on?

I have tried to show you that, even when you make mistakes, all is not lost: you can view them in a positive light and consider them as experiences from which you can learn valuable lessons.

Finally today we considered the range of qualities that make a good decision maker.

**Follow-up**

Look back on a recent decision you made.

1 Did you examine the context, identify the key issues and collect relevant information?
2 Did you identify and evaluate different options?
3 Did you work as a team, implementing and communicating the decision well?
4 What did you do well and what less well?
5 What will you learn for next time and how will you make decisions differently in the future?
6 Looking back at the qualities of a good decision maker, which qualities do you already have and which do you need to cultivate more?

SUNDAY
MONDAY
TUESDAY
WEDNESDAY
THURSDAY
FRIDAY
SATURDAY

# Fact-check [answers at the back]

1. How important is it to evaluate the decision-making process?
   a) Not at all important ❏
   b) Slightly important ❏
   c) Very important for seeing what went well and to learn from mistakes ❏
   d) Useful but only if there is time ❏

2. What will you do when you make a decision in future?
   a) Make a snap decision ❏
   b) Identify and follow through on the different steps I need to take ❏
   c) Muddle through without a formal plan ❏
   d) Do what I've always done ❏

3. What should you be aware of in your role as a decision maker?
   a) My strengths and weaknesses ❏
   b) My strengths ❏
   c) My weaknesses ❏
   d) My strengths and weaknesses in order to tackle my weaknesses ❏

4. What should you do when you make a mistake?
   a) Try to learn from it ❏
   b) Make the same mistake again ❏
   c) Get upset but do nothing ❏
   d) Ignore it ❏

5. What is one key quality of a good decision maker?
   a) Being happy ❏
   b) Decisiveness ❏
   c) Carelessness ❏
   d) Fearfulness ❏

6. If as a manager and decision maker you get absorbed in details, what should you also do?
   a) Stop making progress ❏
   b) Share the ones that fascinate me ❏
   c) I never look at the details ❏
   d) Make sure I also see the big picture ❏

7. What is one of the roles of a manager and decision maker?
   a) To spend more time on social networking websites ❏
   b) To take longer lunch breaks ❏
   c) To communicate a decision clearly ❏
   d) To ignore the needs of colleagues ❏

8. What else does a manager and decision maker need to be?
   a) More punctual at work ❏
   b) Awkward and heavy-handed ❏
   c) Lazy and careless ❏
   d) Discerning and courageous ❏

9. What is the best way to make a difficult decision?

a) Delay making it till the following day, so that I can think it through ('sleep on it') ❏

b) Make it immediately, hoping for the best ❏

c) Delay making it until it's too late ❏

d) Avoid making it ❏

10. As a decision maker, what should your aim be?

a) To stay the same ❏

b) To make my own rules about decision making ❏

c) To be the best decision maker I can be, using this book for reference ❏

d) To remain an average decision maker ❏

# 7 × 7

## 1 Seven key questions to ask yourself

- What am I actually making a decision about?
- In truth, have I already made up my mind or is there a decision to make?
- What are the most influential factors affecting my decision?
- What are the secondary factors affecting my decision?
- Do I have a preferred or an expected outcome?
- What will happen if I make a mistake?
- Do I have all the relevant details to make my decision?

## 2 Seven things to do today

- **Check back:** Remind yourself why you need to make a decision in the first place: think about the context.
- **Get reading:** Immerse yourself in the subject matter as thoroughly as possible, by reading online, in professional journals or books, and by discussing the issues with colleagues.
- **Follow up:** Review the outstanding actions from your last meeting – do you have the latest details, and are there actions still to take before you can reach your conclusion?
- **Risk-assess:** Run through the likely outcomes based on different decisions you might make, and analyse how they would affect your goal.
- **Clear your mind of clutter**: Focus on the decision in hand rather than trying to resolve countless issues all at once.
- **Carry out background research:** Find out what competitors have tried, and why they succeeded or failed.
- **Remember the steps to take:** Start SCAMPERING around and being SMARTER (check them out below).

# 3 Seven things to avoid

- **Appeasement:** Make the right decision because it is the *right* decision, not because it avoids confrontation or extra work.

- **Pig-headedness:** Don't be afraid to change your mind if you're presented with a persuasive and well-judged argument.

- **Data overload:** Detail is great, but don't drown in it. Assess what level of data you need to make an informed decision and focus on that.

- **Issue evasion:** Be direct and tackle issues head on; skirting around them means you will not resolve them.

- **Personal bias:** Yes, red may be your favourite colour, but is it *really* suitable for your business's new toothpaste?

- **Procrastination:** Dithering will get you nowhere... if you're taking your time to make a decision, be sure that you're using that time wisely.

- **Wearing too many hats**: Delegate tasks to those who are best at them, and use their feedback to inform your final decision. You can't be butcher, baker, and candlestick-maker all at once without becoming a knave.

# 4 Seven SMARTER steps to success

- **Specific** – not vague detail
- **Measurable** and quantifiable targets
- **Agreed** decisions with other stakeholders
- **Realistic** and resourced to meet success
- **Timed** actions – no drifting
- **Evaluated** progress and project analysis
- **Reported** progress to all stakeholders

# 5 Seven great qualities for decision makers

- **Balance:** Being able to see multiple angles and assessing them without bias makes you a stronger decision maker.

- **Courage:** Summon your inner strength to follow the path that you've decided upon, even when this is intimidating.

- **Determination:** Don't give up after one small mistake or wrong decision – use it as a learning opportunity.

- **Integrity:** Honesty, transparency and following your principles mean that, no matter what the outcome, you'll earn respect for your approach to decision making.

- **Listening:** One of the greatest tools of communication is the human ear: use it when planning your decision.

- **Strategy:** Seeing the big picture and targeting it without being sidetracked by unnecessary detail can sometimes make even the toughest decision seem simpler.

- **Vision:** Looking beyond your current situation to envisage the best outcome allows you to act with purpose.

# 6 Seven steps to SCAMPER

- **Substitute:** Can you look to swap out a person or process?

- **Combine:** Can you combine two or more parts into one more efficient part?

- **Adapt:** Can you adapt what you already have without reinventing the wheel?

- **Modify:** Can you implement a significant change to your product or process?

- **Put to other use:** Can you use your idea in a completely different way or repurpose it?

- **Eliminate:** Can you trim any excess fat to bring efficiency?

- **Reverse:** Can you swap the order of your processes to make a change for the better?

# 7 Seven inspiring business decisions

- Automobile magnate Henry Ford decided to double the wages of his workforce, enabling him to attract the quality of employee he desired and raising workforce engagement – his employees could afford to buy the cars they were working on.

- Ursula Burns secured the future of Xerox when competitors such as Kodak were falling by the wayside, by moving beyond – or eliminating – traditional products and branching out into hi-tech business solutions for the digital era.

- Apple's board decided to bring Steve Jobs back to the company, a decade after firing him... leading to a stunning change in fortune through innovative products such as the iPod and iPhone.

- Bill Allen persuaded the Boeing board to invest $16 million in developing the Boeing 707, transforming US transatlantic commercial flight from propeller technology to the jet age.

- Never one to be pigeonholed into a single area of commerce, Richard Branson revolutionized the mobile phone sector by introducing prepaid mobiles, listening to the needs of customers rather than following the conventions of his rivals.

- Sport is big business these days, and one of the shrewdest decisions in the modern era of football was made by Lisbon's famous football club, Benfica, which gave virtually unknown former translator José Mourinho his big break in management: he has gone on to countless big leagues and cups, and has won the UEFA Champion's League twice (but, sadly, not with Benfica).

- *Your* next big decision; you have the tools and ability to make the right call, so go for it!

# Answers

**Sunday:** 1d; 2d; 3c; 4b; 5d; 6a; 7c; 8c; 9b; 10b.

**Monday:** 1d; 2b; 3c; 4b; 5d; 6b; 7c; 8a; 9c; 10a.

**Tuesday:** 1a; 2d; 3a; 4a; 5b; 6c; 7d; 8c; 9b; 10b.

**Wednesday:** 1c; 2b; 3d; 4a; 5d; 6d; 7b; 8a; 9c; 10b.

**Thursday:** 1d; 2a; 3b; 4c; 5b; 6b; 7b; 8b; 9c; 10b.

**Friday:** 1b; 2a; 3d; 4c; 5a; 6c; 7b; 8d; 9d; 10b.

**Saturday:** 1c; 2b; 3d; 4a; 5b; 6d; 7c; 8d; 9a; 10c.

# Notes

# ALSO AVAILABLE IN THE 'IN A WEEK' SERIES

For information about other titles in the 'In A Week' series, please visit www.teachyourself.co.uk

# MORE TITLES AVAILABLE IN THE 'IN A WEEK' SERIES

**For information about other titles in the 'In A Week' series, please visit www.teachyourself.co.uk**

**YOUR FASTEST ROUTE
TO SUCCESS**

**LEARN IN A WEEK WHAT
THE EXPERTS LEARN
IN A LIFETIME**

For information about other titles
in the 'In A Week' series, please visit
www.teachyourself.co.uk